DEEP IMAGE

JONES IRWIN

DEEP IMAGE
by Jones Irwin

Copyright © 2025 by Jones Irwin
Published by Tofu Ink Arts Press. All rights reserved.
Edited by Brian L. Jacobs
Book design by JLTY Atelier

Front cover by Gemma Rose

ISBN: 978-1-958661-16-1

Tofu Ink Arts Press, a celebratory venture, aims at publishing
poems and other arts of un humdrum'd inclusive rhizomatic errant
possibilities. We support polished work of established & emerging
poets and artists that are absorbed in possibilities. We are
committed to amplifying voices of the under-represented and
marginalized. Art makes you think about thinking…

ABSORB POSSIBILITIES!

www.TOFUINK.com
A member of CLMP

To Jerome Rothenberg,

for the ANYKINDNESS of poems

Contents

Prose and Longer Poems

Haikus and Shorter Poems

Acknowledgments

The author would like to acknowledge the previous publication of specific poems and prose works in journals and to express appreciation to the various editors for support in the development of the work. This work was originally conceived as a Chapbook but, under the inspiration of Tofu Ink Press, in San Francisco and Malaysia, evolved into a full-length hybrid work. Tofu Ink Press are a wonderful example of the small, independent press and poetry journal, continuing the legacy of the Beats and Naropa University, and I am hugely thankful to Brian Jacobs and Joseph Lee for their support, encouragement and advice, in terms of text and image. Long may Tofu Ink flourish! The original catalyst for this work was the poem 'What Will Happen Then?', included here, which was the winner of the Rez Abdoh 2023 Tofu Ink Poetry Prize.

Small and independent presses are a salvation for the experimental writer. Special thanks also on this score to Larry Robin/Moonstone Arts Centre, to Matthew Bullen and *Red Ogre Review*, to Manuela Irarrazabal and the *Espacio Fronterizo* (*Borderland/ Espace Frontière*) journal, to Dimitri Kaufmann and *The Decadent Review* and to Mignolo Arts Centre/Pinky Thinker Press and Charly Santagado. The striking *Deep Image* cover illustration is by the English artist Gemma Rose, so very special gratitude to Gemma for allowing me to employ it for this publication. Several of her images from the Two-Tone essay are also redeployed here. My son Gregory Campbell Irwin has also contributed the 'Ghost Town' and 'American Haikus' images, much love to talented Greg. A heartfelt thanks to my family and friends for their sustaining love and inspiration.

I acknowledge here the previous publication of the following texts:

'From Bashō's Japanese Verse to Kerouac's "American Haikus"' in *Espacio Fronterizo (Borderland/ Espace Frontière),* June 2024.

'Psychogeography' (earlier version), *Showbear Family Circus* Journal of Liberal Arts, Brooklyn, Autumn 2019. *Espacio Fronterizo (Borderland/ Espace Frontière)*, Summer 2022.

'Moira' (prose poem) in *Tofu Ink Arts Press*, Spring 2021. Edited by Brian L. Jacobs. 'Moira' in *Taint Taint*, July 2022. 'Moira', *Fatal Flaw*, Volume 4, 'Ritual', August 2021. Flash fiction.

'This Italian May' in *Espacio Fronterizo (Borderland/ Espace Frontière)*, April 2023

'Deep Image Or A Painting By Jeffrey Dahmer' in Tofu Ink Press, Summer 2023. 'Deep Image Or A Painting By Jeffrey Dahmer', Mignolo Arts, *Pinky Thinker Press Journal.* October 2023

'Of Western Civilisation', *Havik Literary Journal*, June 2021. Flash fiction.

'Not All Priests Are On The Side Of The Good'. *The Decadent Review*, February 2022.

'After The Death of God - A Fictional Biography of Georges Bataille'. Published *in toto The Decadent Review*, August 2021. Republished *Mignolo Arts Pinky Thinker Press* (journal) Issue 5, January 2022.

'What Will Happen Then?'. *Espacio Fronterizo (Borderland/Espace Frontière)*, Summer 2022. Winner of Rez Abdoh 2023 Tofu Ink Poetry Prize.

'Who Killed Gilles Deleuze? – Episode 1'. *The Decadent Review*, Summer 2022.

Irwin, Jones and Rose, Gemma. 'Coventry *Haiku* - Two-Tone Poetics and the Psychogeography of Ska'. *Red Ogre Review*, June 2024.

'Thessaloniki Student Revolt Haikus' in *WILDSOUND* Writing Festival, August 2024.

'Lucifer Haikus' in 'Poetics of Hell – From Arthur Rimbaud and Sartre to the Voidoids' in *Red Ogre Review*, Lancaster, UK. October 2024.

'Verlaine/Television Haikus' in *'Parallèlement* - From Paul Verlaine and Symbolism to Tom Verlaine and *Television'*, *Red Ogre Review*, Lancaster, UK. August 2024.

'Francis Bacon Study#1', Tofu Ink Press, January 2022.

'The Coach and Horses', *In Parentheses*, April 2021.

'The Librarian', *In Parentheses*, April 2021.

'Portrait de Madeleine Riffaud', Moonstone Poetry Ink Annual Anthology, Autumn 2024, Philadelphia, US.

'Tragic Optimism'. Freedom Moonstone Anthology Summer 2024.Philadelphia, US.

'The Pluralist School' in *Espacio Fronterizo (Borderland/ Espace Frontière)*, Autumn 2024.

'My Hands Are A City' (plus *Compositional Note*). Mignolo, Pinky Thinker Press, New Jersey, April 2025.

'Housmans Bookshop Haiku'. Tofu Ink Press, Volume7.

'Bealach Níos Fearr Chun Cónaí/Better Way To Live – The Irish Language Hip Hop Poetics Of *Kneecap'*. *Red Ogre Review*, February 2025. Lancaster, UK.

'Participation' and 'Beauty is in the Street' images, in Vermès, P. & Kugelberg, J. (Eds.). (2011). *La beauté est dans la rue. Beauty Is In The Street. A Visual Record of the May '68 Paris Uprising*. London: Four Corners Books.

A Short Introduction After Rothenberg

'For us, Jerome Rothenberg played (and plays) the role Picasso and Braque did for the painters, and Leiris and Bataille later for the French poets: opening the sparkling world that comes when you crack open literature and see the primal gestures of oral energy and sudden imagery from which it all surges' (Robert Kelly)

Deep Image is originally Jerome Rothenberg's conception. Through this vision of experimental writing, he shakes up received ideas of what poems ought to be like. In this full-length work of prose and poetry, I have sought to operationalise this philosophy of *l'écriture* (also with a tip of the beret to Jacques Derrida), juxtaposing metafiction texts with prose poems, haikus and shorter verse. As for Rothenberg, my own practice as a philosopher brings me to seek out and to create texts which bear a relation to the complex human condition as a deeper presence restructuring the poem and poetics.

In our times of contemporary crisis, it is hoped that the writing of poetry and of poetics, as a kind of *minor literature*, might serve and supplicate as a surprisingly robust resource contra the banality of mainstream culture (whether Spotify, FB or worse). I have also included a recent critical text as Preface, which draws out the genealogy of an ethical and aesthetic counter-culture all the way from the ancient culture of Bashō to our current malaise.

Jones Irwin, Dublin, October 2025.

"You should quench violence more quickly than a fire"
- Heraclitus

Critical Poetics Essays

From Bashō's Japanese Verse to Kerouac's 'American Haikus'

'Looking up at the stars/feeling sad/Going "tsk, tsk, tsk"'
(Kerouac 2004).

Although the tradition of 'haiku' poetry was already well established in Japan by the birth of Matsuo Kinsaku in 1644, it was this specific poet who would reinvigorate the form. Changing his name to Bashō after the nickname given him by his disciples, the word for a banana tree with big soft leaves, his evolution of the haiku already took it beyond the originally prescriptive seventeen syllable count (Stryk 1985). Bashō took a throughgoing approach to poetry, seeing it as a way of life, connecting a disavowal of possessions with a vow of poverty and incessant travel to the writing of poems which sought to allow the objecthood of things to speak for themselves. The brevity and curtness of the haiku form was perfectly suited to this task, avoiding ostentatious verbal or conceptual complexity. This aesthetic and existential vision for Bashō was grounded in a philosophy or religion of Zen Buddhism: 'like other haiku poets of his time, Bashō considered himself a Zennist, indeed was thought to be a Zen monk' (Stryk 1985: 15).

This Zen philosophy carried certain values with it which founded the poetic practice. First of all, a 'lightness' (*karumi*) which indicated a detachment or commitment to non-attachment which allowed for the poem to be free of weightiness. Second, this lightness went in hand with solitariness or *sabi*, from people and from worldly goods, which allows for the freedom of the wandering poet (Bashō travelled extensively). Finally, *wabi* or the 'spirit of poverty' enabled Bashō to live simply and frugally, in an infamous 'hut', a dwelling of peace. Although traditional in following these tenets of the Zen Buddhist framework, Bashō experimented with the syllable count to break with the prescriptive aspects and also wrote prose, taking the form of *haibun* (prose followed by haiku), which was concrete and imagistic (Stryk 1985: 15).

Bashō's own haiku poems seek to capture each of these elements in the most simple and sparse of forms, a three-line count. Two of his haikus here show this form at its most succinct yet expressive, capturing also the connection between minor events and the reference to the macrocosm or the wider 'timeless and universal spirit'.

On the dead limb

squats a crow –

autumn night.

Spring air –

woven moon

and plum scent.

(Bashō 1985: 11)

We here see the shift between the micro- and the macro-, the specific and the universal, and these two elements of the haiku form (the condition/situation and then the sudden perception) are divided by a break (*kireji*, or 'cutting word', 'best rendered in English by emphatic punctuation' (Stryk 1985: 11)).

Bashō's own adherence to the tradition while simultaneously breaking with it is instructive in coming to explore the emergence of Jack Kerouac's interpretation of the possibilities of the poetic form. In many respects, the Beat sensibility and aesthetic vision (with Kerouac as a paradigm figure) represents a continuation of specific tenets of the Japanese strain of writing whilst applied to a very different culture of mid-twentieth century America.

Whereas the classical concept of haiku is the three-line, seventeen syllable Japanese poetic form, Kerouac experimented with this genre, taking it beyond strict syllable counts into what he believed was the form's essence. This *American haiku* (so called) was then incorporated into his correspondence, notebooks, journals, sketchbooks and readings, further blurring the lines between poetry, prose and spoken word. He even embeds haikus in lists of street addresses. It is this looser, more dexterous, haiku form which I have sought to deploy in my own recent poems included in this Chapbook. Although the word haiku is singular and plural, Kerouac uses the word 'haikus', which is unusual (no doubt indicating thereby his more differentiated and pluralist vision for the genre). I follow Kerouac in this usage.

Despite this differentiated conception, Kerouac's definition of the renewed haiku is simple enough (quoted Weinreich 2004: x): 'I propose that the "Western Haiku" simply say a lot in three short lines in any Western language. Above all, a Haiku must be very simple and free of all poetic trickery and make a little picture and yet be as airy and graceful as a Vivaldi Pastorella'.

Traditional haiku collections are organized by season or by subject. In taking the classical form beyond the classical Japanese categorisation, Kerouac's own vision for the genre is multi-layered. Specific sub-forms emerge in his deployment of the genre. What he calls 'pops' are philosophical short poems while 'beat generation haikus' are more angry and emotionally blunt renditions. His usage of the form is directed towards capturing a subject's essence while paradoxically denoting the ephemeral nature of fleeting existence and what Weinreich refers to as the 'sensitivity to impermanence'. This is rendered powerfully in the image (which is also part of the traditional haiku vision) of an isolated figure in a broader landscape, 'One flower/on the cliffside/nodding at the canyon' (quoted Weinreich 2004: xvii), this isolation being a kind of quintessential Kerouacean (as well as outsider American) persona.

Other significant features of this version of 'American Haikus' are the visual possibilities of poetry, which were

15

connected to Kerouac's own use of spontaneous or automatic prose, as well as his habit of sketching drawings alongside his writings. Of course, there is also a paradox to this link to automatism, as these short poems are extra-disciplined and it is clear that Kerouac often rewrote and revised them over a long period of time The same can be said more generally about his writing, including the mythic prose (*On the Road* etc.), which were hardly automatic works in the one sitting as mythologised but often prose works created over significant periods of temporal revision. One often finds these new fangled 'haikus' embedded in the longer works (including in *On The Road*), complicating the relation between the prose and the poetry.

With regard to the visual aspect as such, we are exhorted to 'WRITE *HAIKUS* THEN PAINT THE SCENE DESCRIBING THEM'. Here, there is an interesting emergence of the distinction between describing and 'looking', where haikus may be more like paintings than other genres of poems in being more to do with 'looking' than 'describing'. There is also the sense that *haikus* can themselves be 'looked at', that is the haiku may itself be akin to a painting or a visual object (sometimes, first and foremost before we read it or seek to understand its semantic meaning). Moreover, there is a kind of 'purposeful cut' (or 'caesura') characteristic of this form of writing, both in its classical and more 'American' form and this is often linked to incongruous juxtapositions which rather than being spontaneous, need to be 'best reworked and revised' (quoted Weinreich 2004: xix).

This emphasis on revision and on discipline with regard to this renewed form of poetics also has a spiritual dimension. This is hardly surprising in that the original Japanese form is linked intrinsically to meditation and to Zen Buddhism, as we saw with Bashō. *Haiku* composition is a matter of discipline, as difficult to achieve as spending time in Zen meditation (this also links to Kerouac's own interest in Buddhism which was more literary than religious, as it was in the latter understanding for other related American poets of the time such as Gary Snyder). Kerouac here found aesthetic and emotive sympathies rather than anything metaphysical: 'Buddhism stayed a literary concern for him, not a meditative or spiritual practice as it was for Snyder and Whalen' (Weinreich 2004: xiv). Moreover, wasn't this reconstruction of the overarching and fundamental vision also intrinsic to his successful transformation of the 'haiku' (Buddhist, Japanese, classical etc.) into his own, original version of the all-new 'American haikus? This is also a connecting bridge between Kerouac and other avant-garde poetic schools which were emerging or which would further emerge in the next decade. For example, it brings Kerouac closer to the Black Mountain School than his Beat contemporaries as well as proximate in spirit to the (American) urbanity of New York School poets such as Frank O'Hara, whose urbane poems nonetheless evoked also (often in their succinctness and deceptive simplicity, above all else) the conception of 'American haikus', which Kerouac originally envisioned.

Hail Jack Keroauc then, originator of effectively a new and very dexterous poetic form, with classical connections and inspiration but with a contemporary edge, bridging and hybridizing rural and urban, individual and collective, humorous irony and painful seriousness. And here, we might argue this vision can be of inspiration again to us budding philosophical-poet types. And we also continue to break its inherent rules and extend it a little, as a genre and a form – why not, dear reader? Please find below some of my experiments in this endeavour.

Here I include a short selection of my own American haikus (or is there an Irish specific sub-category of such?), the first which obeys the seasonal or nature reference , the second which takes up Kerouac's 'pops' or personal-philosophical thematics, the third the more emotionally blunt 'beat generation haiku' concept, the fourth which comes from a series of 'Coventry haikus' (connecting to Ska music) and the last which plays with a naughty extension of the classic 3 line limit, if nothing else ('Dublin City Blues'):

*****

Fresh Pure Lake Haiku

By God this lake

Is a haiku

Japhy in his swim shorts

Deleuze Haiku

According to Gilles

Kerouac was a Crack Up

Dharma Bum Asylum

Beat Generation Haiku

I found a crushed snake

On a Spanish walk

Who's soul baulked?

Coventry Haiku

Midlands David Lynch

Isabella Rossellini phone

Calling Terry Hall

Dublin City Blues

After Jack Kerouac

Got up & dressed up

    & went out & got paid

Then came home & got laid

    in a mauve suit in the garden

Man –

    we feign perfection

Because we are empty

Because feigning is a

    kind of emptiness

Because it is a kind of perfection

(Irwin 2024).

References

Bashō (1985) *On Love and Barley – Haiku of Bashō*. Penguin Books, London.

Irwin, Jones (2023) '#American *Haiku*' in *Red Ogre Review*, September 2023. Lancaster, England.

Kerouac, Jack (2004) *Book of Haikus*. Edited and with an Introduction by Regina Weinreich. Enitharmon Press, London.

Stryk, Lucien (1985) 'Introduction' in Basho (1985) *On Love and Barley – Haiku of Basho*. Penguin Books, London.

Weinreich, Regina (2004) 'Introduction: The Haiku Poetics of Jack Kerouac' in Kerouac, Jack (2004) *Book of Haikus*. Edited and with an Introduction by Regina Weinreich. Enitharmon Press, London.

Coventry Haiku - Two-Tone Poetics and the Psychogeography of Ska

'Coventry endlessly tumbles and rebuilds, continually and brutally tears down vistas you've grown up with to build monstrosities you're not prepared for, always destabilises and renders perilous any kind of psychogeography you might want to throw around it' (Kulkarni 2022).

I lived in Coventry, England, for five years between 1994 and 1999. I had left Dublin to study for a PhD in Philosophy at University of Warwick, which at the time was a hot bed of cutting-edge contemporary French thought, led by the maverick theorist of nihilism Nick Land who was originally meant to be my thesis supervisor although he turned my work down for being 'too medievalist' (Land resigned his post before I left the university, going on to become a guru of the Alt-Right). This wasn't the first time this apparently bland Midlands mid-sized city had captured the *zeitgeist*. Back in the late 1970s, Coventry was the specific site of the emergence of British Ska and Two-Tone, a music and cultural-political movement which married hybrid sounds to a progressive anti-racist ideology. The tentacles of this movement spread far and wide, reaching even my own neighbourhood in Northside Dublin when the Ska bands played an infamous gig at the *Stardust* nightclub, two weeks before a tragic fire on Valentine's Night which was to claim the lives of 48 romantic teens. I tried to capture this strange juxtaposition in the title poem of my first Chapbook, entitled *Ghost Town*:

Ghost Town

I

Last time was this quiet
Northside after they
took the bodies from the
Stardust right round the corner
from Beaumont hospital.

Two weeks earlier *The Beat*
and *The Specials* played a Ska tour
date and Jayo's mates caused a
riot Terry Hall nearly died when
a giant speaker just missed his head.
(Irwin 2022).

The *Stardust* tragedy represented a crisis-point for us Northsiders, growing up in the working-class suburbs now blighted by an irresolvable trauma. Several of my school friends in Coolock had lost older siblings in the torrid fire, some of whose bodies remained unidentified for decades. I remember vividly the aftershocks of this event, the tendency to random and/or reactive violence amongst some of my damaged peers, their psychic distress, the atmosphere of total disenfranchisement, the sense of school and education (and the workplace which might follow on) being some kind of spectral hallucination without meaning, reduced to bleak absurdity. Even if I belonged only in an ancillary or indirect way to the epicentre of this existential drama, one nonetheless saw the uncaring hypocrisy of a wider society all too clearly and unequivocally. This truly was a lost generation of youth, thrown into the abyss without any real concern for the consequences (and the effects would manifest later in violence, in a criminal underworld and elsewhere). One imagines a very different approach taken if this had been a middle-class neighbourhood but it was precisely this forsaken social and psychic alienation which bridged the gap between Coolock on the one side and Foleshill, Hillfields and Tile Hill in the late 1970s, between Dublin and Coventry. Somehow Ska music and lyrics, emerging in the English Midlands but already transported from a (Jamaican) elsewhere, seemed to speak so eloquently and so compassionately to our mutual predicament.

We were all experiencing what Iain Sinclair has referred to as a great rift between language and the material (political) environment. In a review of Sinclair's Collected Poems, *Firewall*, Robert Bond has spoken of this as precisely 'the collapse of our civic morality and ambition – a powerful downshift in consciousness of the 1980s and 1990s…the victim of rogue-capitalist relativism: nil by mouth indeed' (Bond 2008). Sinclair's poetry works connect to his later (and more well known) psychogeography of London and its environs, what Bond refers to as 'the ghost – the afterburn – of a written urban life; and even also the skeleton of a re-born, spiritual expressive life' (Bond 2008). This is where such a psychogeography allows us to access a 'spiritual topography', writing and philosophising from 'the map of another world altogether'.

In recent short articles for *Red Ogre Review* (Irwin 2022, 2023, 2024a), I have sought to draw out the contours of a poetics which might do justice to such a contemporary psychogeography. Building on Jack Kerouac's more urbane evolution of the traditional Japanese *haiku* form, I drew out a novel experimentation with this classical form where Keroauc claimed to have taken the 'American *haikus*' beyond strict syllable counts or prescriptive content into the 'form's essence' (Irwin 2023): 'I propose that the "Western *Haiku*" simply say a lot in three short lines in any Western language' (quoted Weinreich 2004: x). With reference to sources such as John Cooper Clarke and Jim Carroll (via Kurt Cobain), I pictured an emergent conception of 'punk *haikus*', which might do the (spiritual and political) job required for us today (Irwin 2023, 2024a).

What specific lessons might my auto-narrative of Midlands days and the juxtaposition of Coventry and Dublin via Ska poetics have for this ongoing story? Today as I write this (Thursday, 18th April 2024, 13.57pm, in a Birmingham café), a long overdue governmental enquiry[1] in Ireland into the *Stardust* tragedy is edging towards its final verdicts. Life always seems to have a way of moving on, while constantly looking over its shoulder at the tragic and the unresolved. In December 2022, that arch-poet of Ska, Terry Hall, died, bringing on a whole avalanche of reminisces and retrospective reinterpretations for those of who followed in his inspiring slipstream.

The poet David R. Mellor captured some of this collective grief in his poem titled simply 'Terry Hall', a short excerpt here:

I heard the news
At 4.30 a.m. exactly
I knew it would hurt
And it did so badly

A voice that blew away the fluff of the 80's
A sincere stare
And words that were rich and plenty…

An honesty that left you feeling less alone
A life of pain
etched in words that could have been my own

I heard the news
At 4.30 a.m. exactly
I knew it would hurt
And it did so badly

---

[1] As I concluded this essay, Irish news *RTE* announced a verdict of 'unlawful killing' for the 48 victims of *The Stardust* (18.04.24 15.04pm).

(Mellor 2022).

A related article in *The Quietus* by the music journalist Neil Kulkarni similarly grasped the psychogeography of Hall's artistic achievements, alongside his *Specials* compatriots and the wider Ska movement. Entitled 'Coventry and a Spirit of Unbelonging: Terry Hall Remembered' (Kulkarni 2022), Kulkarni disavows Philip Larkin, also a Coventrian, in favour of Hall as *the* Coventry poet: 'in the death of Terry Hall, we have lost our greatest ever poet' (Kulkarni 2022). For Kulkarni, it is the voice and the visage of Hall ('mordant, still faintly smiling, never quite sneering') which balances or mixes a spirit of 'resignation and resistance…a city of bombs and rebirth…[where] medieval and modernist are crushed together so abrasively' (Kulkarni 2022).

Between Coventry and Dublin, then, and between the upcoming *Stardust* verdict and the looking back at Terry Hall the poet, I would like to suggest that the contours of a psychogeography[2] emerge which can draw on the *haiku* (especially in its Kerouacian 'American *haikus*' version) and on the Two-Tone poetry of Ska. Let me conclude with some short, sharp shock renditions of my own which we might classify under a 'Coventry *haikus*' banner. I am currently preparing a collection of these succinct texts[3].

----

[2] One of my first published poems was entitled *Psychogeography* and emerged from a certain, hallucinatory experience of Coventry via Dublin. I have included the poem in Prose and Longer Poems section of this text.

[3] Special thanks to the English artist Gemma Rose for the illustrations which accompany this text.

Two-Tone Poetics, No.1

30 years later
Two-Tone loos
Less smell of piss

Midlands David Lynch
Isabella Rossellini phone call
Calling Terry Hall

Goth in Covid mask
Bald with stringy beard
Is there no God?

Two-Tone Poetics, No. 2

Missed Ska beat
The Stardust burned
No one paid

Lower Precinct all sparkle
Natives still shout WANKER
At flashy new consumers

Jerry Dammers' hair
Gets stranglier yearly
He channels elves

Sex games at Canley
The Crematorium sighs
Love is an ideology

Train station dust
Rises to meet
Incoming Birmingham

Two-Tone Poetics, No. 3

George Shaw canvas
In the Tile Hill woods
With music by *The Selecter*

At Berkswell
The swans choke
On the ennui of Myth

Old Ska dudes
Wearing safari shirts
Discussing neo-racism

References

Bond, Robert (2008) 'Babylon Afterburn: Adventures in Iain Sinclair's *The Firewall*, *Jacket*, Early 2008.

Carroll, Jim (1993) *Fear of Dreaming. The Selected Poems of Jim Carroll*. Penguin, New York.

Carroll, Jim (1994) '8 Fragments For Kurt Cobain'. Louisville, KY: White Fields Press/ The Literary Renaissance, 1994.

Irwin, Jones (2022) 'Ghost Town' in Ghost Town (Chapbook) Moonstone Press, Philadelphia, August 2022.

Irwin, Jones (2023) '#American *Haiku*' in *Red Ogre Review*, September 2023. Lancaster, England.

Irwin, Jones (2024a) 'Jim Carroll Channelling The Suicide of Kurt Cobain – Another Angle On Punk Poetics Via Rothenberg'. *Red Ogre Review*, January 2024

Kerouac, Jack (2004) *Book of Haikus*. Edited and with an Introduction by Regina Weinreich. Enitharmon Press, London.

Kulkarni, Neil (2022) 'Coventry and a Spirit of Unbelonging: Terry Hall Remembered' Hall' in The Quietus, December 2022.

Mellor, D.R. (2022) 'Terry Hall' in The Quietus, December 2022.

Stryk, Lucien (1985) 'Introduction' in Basho (1985) *On Love and Barley – Haiku of Basho*. Penguin Books, London.

Weinreich, Regina (2004) 'Introduction: The Haiku Poetics of Jack Kerouac' in Kerouac, Jack (2004) *Book of Haikus*. Edited and with an Introduction by Regina Weinreich. Enitharmon Press, London.

The Pluralist School

'World is crazier and more of it than we think/ Incorrigibly plural. I peel and portion/ A tangerine and spit the pips and feel/ The drunkenness of things being various' (Louis Mac Niece - ' Snow').

From 2015-2019, I was seconded as Project Officer on the first state curriculum in values and multi-belief education for primary schools in Ireland (there are currently 29 such Community National Schools). Originally, back in 2008/09, these schools had been set up as 'emergency schools', opened to cater for a constituency of children who couldn't find a place in the Catholic dominated primary system. Most of the children concerned were from international/immigrant backgrounds, newly arrived in the Republic of Ireland and falling foul of the 'Catholics first' policy of school enrolment.

For more than a decade previously, I had been involved (as a philosopher of education) in advocating for the need for change in the Irish system, where even today 96% of our primary schools are denominationally run. Specific colleagues and I fought over several years for transformation of the teacher education system and for related change at the level of schooling, and at the heart of this philosophical and values-led movement was a vision of affirmation of difference (rather than fear of the latter), *a saying yes to pluralism*. In this short essay, I will explore how this political and educational project also had deep aesthetic allegiances, and how we might think about the relation between education and literature *across borders*, most particularly the form of poetry and poetics.

Figure 1 Community National Schools in the Republic of Ireland follow the *Goodness Me, Goodness You* curriculum which is the first multi-belief and values curriculum in the history of the state. There are now 29 such state schools across the country.

MacNiece's poem *Snow* (excerpt included above as an epigram) became a continuing recourse for me during this period. But its more primitive evocation of the experience of (natural) difference – 'the drunkenness of things being various' - needed a more formal scaffold to defend an application to education and pedagogy. Bhikhu Parekh's work (Parekh 2005) has been at the heart of the UK and international debate on pluralism in education and the wider society over the last two decades. His groundbreaking text, *Rethinking Multiculturalism*, foregrounds some of the key issues of tension in the problematic of 'multiculturalism'.

'Multicultural societies throw up problems that have no parallel in history. They need to find ways of reconciling unity and diversity, being inclusive without being assimilationist, cherishing plural cultural identities without weakening the precious identity of shared citizenship' (Parekh 2005).

Being inclusive without being assimilationist - schools are often the first interface for this experience of multiculturalism, in that the segregated housing policy for immigrants which is put forward by most Western governments means that children tend to meet across cultures and difference first in school, rather than home community. Policy makers often underestimate the nuance and subtlety required, let us say the *artistry* required, to translate this vision into a school context. As Terence Mc Laughlin notes, 'a school is engaged in a practical enterprise of great complexity which calls for many forms of practical knowledge' (Mc Laughlin 2008: 204).

While challenging, this provides a great possibility for our education systems to lead the way on a more positive and affirmative understanding and practice. In this context, we can foreground *The Pluralist School* as a concept and as an aspiration. In my work in teacher-education, I tend to employ examples from Art to explore perceptions and pre-conceptions of students. The Action-Painting of Jackson Pollock is an evocative resource, beginning with an image of him working on a large blank canvas, across the studio floor. This is life and school as *tabula rasa*, blank slate, open to fresh ideas and experimentation. Of course, this image is somewhat utopian in that contexts are rarely free of original bias or prejudice, often an inherent bias on behalf of the native vs the newcomer (although it can also be the other way, mistrust of the native).

Figure 2 Jackson Pollock in the midst of Action Painting

As a more realistic picture of endemic tensions, I deploy an etching from Goya, *As If They Were Another Breed*, depicting in stark division the exploitation of the Spanish people (subjugated, starved, in some cases to death) by their French colonial masters. This leads to discussion on political division, issues of racism in education and power dynamics between oppressor and oppressed. As a third complicating image, I introduce Pollock's powerful canvas from the '50s, *Convergence*. This expresses an organic unity and harmony which emerges from within an affirmation of difference (and sometimes disharmony). Here we have an artistic representation for the concepts of Parekh – 'cherishing plural cultural identities without weakening the precious identity of shared citizenship' (Parekh 2005).

We might also think of Pollock as leading us back to MacNiece and the more tense ambiguous harmony of *Snow* - 'World is crazier and more of it than we think/ Incorrigibly plural'. But despite the tensions of the situation we faced in the Irish context, the work with Community National Schools was quite the success. There are now, in 2024, 29 such schools in the Republic of Ireland, staffed by capable and visionary teachers and principals, backed by newly confident communities, redeveloping the sense of what education and identity means in Twenty-First century Ireland. One of the stories we employed in the curriculum development was Maurice Sendak's *Where the Wild Things Are*. Michael Rosen has noted how this book was repressed (banned) in the UK for several years after its original publication in the United States: 'at a surface level, this was on account of it being deemed too frightening for very young children, but perhaps they also sensed that it was a book which showed a child's destructive feelings without these feelings being punished'.

While agreeing with Rosen (whose vision of progressive education and childhood is to be lauded), we might also say there is more than destruction in Sendak's children. We perhaps should take some courage from the central child figure Max, in this text:

And when he came to the place where the wild things are

they roared their terrible roars and gnashed their terrible teeth

and rolled their terrible eyes and showed their terrible claws

till Max said "BE STILL!"

and tamed them with the magic trick

of staring into all their yellow eyes without blinking once

and they were frightened and called him the most wild thing of all

and made him king of all wild things.

If we are looking to examples of this vision deployed in more contemporary times, where we confront the monsters of our innermost and primal fears, as individuals and as communities , we can perhaps cite the example in literature of a certain *psychogeography*. This concept originates with the Situationist (and Lettrist) understanding of psychogeography, emerging with the French theorist Guy Debord (seminal for the May '68 events), as 'the study of the specific effects of the geo-graphical environment, consciously organised or not, on the emotions and behaviour of individuals' (quoted Coverley 2006: 10). As Merlin Coverley notes, 'psychogeography is, as the name suggests, the point at which psychology and geography collide, a means of exploring the behavioural impact of urban place' (Coverley 2006: 10). There is also a cultural and philosophical debt here to Surrealism and to Dadaism (earlier to the Symbolism of Rimbaud and Baudelaire), a debt which accrues also up to the Punk movement in music and in literature, which similarly deploys this 'psycho-' or 'damned' dynamic (Hell 2008). This methodology becomes a conducive technique for artists and writers to develop a new philosophical practice of everyday life, and literature (metafiction, poetics etc) becomes a particular pathway to explore. Thus, we find ourselves within a pluralist literary context, enabling various perspectives and lenses on our perception of the world, seeking to work against what Eric Fromm used to call the 'fear of freedom'.

We have examples of how this radical aesthetic has translated very successfully and powerfully into everyday practice, from relatively recent history. Guy Debord's vision was indeed seminal for the May '68 events. His presence as an intellectual subversive at the University of Nanterre on the outskirts of Paris (under the reciprocal tutelage of luminaries such as Henri Lefebvre and Jean Francois Lyotard no less) was a crucial catalyst for the '68 events. The slogans and posters of '68 may be simple, but this is also deceptive. We should rather look to the importance of the political ideas expressed aesthetically as having immediate impact in the late 1960s, but also at the insight of the underlying Situationist philosophy which influenced them. We need to remember the contemporary significance of Situationist theory, especially in the context of the renewal of Marxist thought in the 21st century. This renewed Leftist critique of capitalism emerges as articulated through newer social and political movements of the current times, particularly through the political philosophy of Slavoj Žižek and his auto-critique of the Former Yugoslavia. It remains especially relevant in our present times of crisis and social apocalypse (I write this text on the cusp of the American Presidential Elections in early November 2024).

But the avowal of a critique of ideology also comes with a significant philosophical health warning from the Situationists and this is a self-satire that is also prominent in '68 and again visible in the posters. 'Participation - All the Better to Eat You With My Children!' (Vermès & Kugelberg, 2011, p. 6).

Figure 3 Participation - All the Better to Eat You With My Children! Reprinted from Vermès & Kugelberg (2011: 6)

How the dream of emancipation and the empowerment of the underclass (or 'the children' here as another example of infantilism) runs aground! Perhaps all this talk of increasing radicalisation and democratisation ('we are so much more radical than you are' or ''Oh look at how pluralist our school is'!) may be just alternate ruses to co-opt any potentially transformative action into complicity with the forces of power. This poster and this declaration also contains an angry and somewhat disillusioned question; what then would

44

authentic participation in the revolution be, what would it look like? What could it possibly feel like in the real world beyond the spectacle? Is there even such a place, today, in 2024?

Freire thinks there is such a Utopia of pluralism (and a possible real-time school) and describes it thus: 'the creation of multiculturality; it calls for a certain educational practice. It calls for a new ethics, founded on respect for differences, a unity in differences' (Freire 1992: 137). Is it too much to suggest that our own Community National Schools in Ireland might have been one group of such (29) experiments, in this case doing quite well, thank you very much?

This is certainly a vision we would like to endorse. But its achievement cannot be smooth or linear. In present times, the emergence of change and of authentic participation will not be easily won. It will require protest and revolt. To conclude this particular essay, I add a series of *haiku* I developed under the inspiration of another such related but particular context of struggle and critique, the context of student protest in Thessaloniki, Greece. I visited Thessaloniki in July 2024 and interviewed the main student leaders and we are currently developing a book project on their vision for a renewed and public (state) University in Greece *contra* the forces which seek to reify education into a commodity for sale. I came away inspired by their energy, vision and affirmative joy in revolt (also their humour and generosity of spirit) and wrote the *haiku* in tribute. Their ideas and their practice show how we might connect a vision of the pluralist school to the pluralist university and, of course, to an authentically multicultural and (unfearful) differentiated society. *La Lutte Continue*.

Figure 4 Repainting of Picasso's *Guernica* by AntiCapitalist Students Thessaloniki, hanging in The Rectory, Aristotle Thessaloniki University, Greece, July 2024.

Student Revolt Thessaloniki Haikus[4]

I interviewed Alexis

Who told me about riots

-     against the privatised University

At Aristotle Thessaloniki

Anarchists stage an occupation

-     no to commercial education

Students repainted *Guernica*

To avoid the same fate

-     it hangs in the Rectorate

---

[4] Mignolo Arts/Pinky Thinker Press in New Jersey, US have developed an inter-disciplinary translation of this *haiku* which also evinces a concern for borders and border-disciplinary crossings. Thanks to Mignolo and especially to Charly Santagado for their inspiring work on this. This work evinces a pluralist form of literature or a pluralist iteration of what Jacques Derrida called '*l'écriture*'. For the Mignolo shared performance of the *haiku*, see here: https://www.mignolo.art/convosintranslation/jonesirwin.

AntiCapitalists gather in the Steki

Iced coffee for the Revolution

- caffeine helps with enlightenment

In the city it hits 38 degrees

The Gaza demo does Aristotelous

- black and red flags rise

Petros sees an uncertain future

Tales of hurt and of exploitation

- oppression without redemption

Together we read Kropotkin

Later Marx and Bakunin

- literature is a burning sun

Aliki thinks I'm mad

To think this at Halkidiki

- student revolt will win out

(Irwin 2025).

References

Boroditskaya, Marina and Rosen, Michael (2015) "Children's Poetry and Politics: A Conversation," in Dugdale, ed., *Modern Poetry in Translation*, 67-74.

Coverley, Merlin (2006) *Psychogeography*. Oldcastle Books, London.

Freire, P. (1996). *Pedagogy of the Oppressed*. London: Continuum

Irwin, Jones (2016) 'Aesthetic-Ethical-Religious: Goodness Me! Goodness You! Curriculum With A Nod To Where The Wild Things Are' in *Breac. A Digital Journal of Irish Studies*. University of Notre Dame, USA.

Irwin, Jones (2025) *Deep Image*. Tofu Ink Press, California, USA.

Mac Niece, Louis (2002) *Collected Poems*. Penguin. London.

Mc Laughlin, T.H. (2008) 'The Burdens and Dilemmas of Common Schooling' in Carr, D, Halstead, M and Pring, R. (eds) *Liberalism, Education and Schooling, Essays by T.H.Mc Laughlin* (2008) Imprint, Exeter.

Parekh, B. (2005) *Rethinking Multiculturalism*. Routledge, London.

Sendak, Maurice (2000) *Where the Wild Things Are* (New York: Random House)

Vermès, P. & Kugelberg, J. (Eds.). (2011). *La beauté est dans la rue*. London

Žižek, S. (1989). *The Sublime Object of Ideology*. London: Verso.

Bealach Níos Fearr Chun Cónaí/Better Way To Live –
The Irish Language Hip Hop Poetics Of *Kneecap*

'Faoi dheireadh tá deireadh tagtha le mo rut/Mar bhí lá maith agamsa inniu, buíochas le foc' (Finally my rut has ended/Because I had a good day today, thank fuck) – Kneecap *Better Way To Live*

'Gach focal a labhraítear i nGaeilge… is é piléar scaoilte ar son saoirse na hÉireann' (Every word of Irish spoken.. it is a bullet for Irish freedom) - Arló Ó Cairealláin (*Kneecap* film 2024)

'Tráthnóna na teangan in Éirinn/Is an oíche ag bogthitim mar scéal' (Late evening for the language in Ireland/With night falling softly as a story') – Seán Ó'Ríordáin *Do Dhomhnall Ó Corcora* (For Daniel Corkery))

Speaking about the poetry of Jerome Rothenberg, Robert Kelly states that, for his generation of outsider poets, Rothenberg 'played the role Picasso did for the painters… opening the sparkling world that comes when you crack open literature and see the primal gestures of oral energy and sudden imagery from which it all surges' (Kelly quoted in Rothenberg 2013). This conception of *a primal oral energy* from which literature derives is a significant thesis when one explores the specific case of Irish literature. The history of Irish literature includes the poetries of two languages, one in Irish (or Gaeilge) and the other in English, both with strong roots in the oral traditions of narrative and verse. Oftentimes, these two languages intersect and co-operate, at times of course also they end up in sectarian conflict (most notably, during the British colonial period of Irish history, when the Irish language was suppressed). Much has been written about this complex history, but more recently a somewhat unlikely example of such cross-fertilisation has emerged in Northern Ireland; the Irish language Hip Hop poetics of the band (from Belfast and Derry), *Kneecap* (Kneecap 2024).

In the semi-fictional docu comedy drama about their emergence, also simply entitled *Kneecap* (Peppiatt 2024) and directed by the English director Rich Peppiatt, one of the characters realises that, on being questioned by the police, an Irish-language speaker can demand to have an Irish-language translator, fundamentally changing the dynamic of any such police interrogation and potentially any relationship between language per se and the police/the state itself. In this moment, the very relation between English and Irish oral languages is foregrounded, and the irremediable (legal and coercive) tension between them. As Peter Bradshaw has noted, 'Kneecap have been a blazingly fierce presence since they emerged from the Irish language movement in the North, reinventing the political purpose of hip-hop and fighting a rearguard action for republican and Irish culture against a somnolent consensus.. a day after (Prince) William and Kate's royal visit to the city's Empire Music Hall, they showed up there doing a gig that involved raucously shouting (in English) "Brits out"' (Bradshaw 2024). In the film, this bluntly anti-British sentiment phrase appears daubed on the pallid bum cheeks of one of the protagonists, as he bends over on front of the baying crowd to make his political statement for Irish freedom and unity. As his girlfriend (previously unaware of his involvement, as his face is disguised in an Irish nationalist tricolor balaclava) later notes; 'I recognised your lovely arse on TV'.

The three members of the band, Mo Chara, Móglaí Bap and cheeky arse DJ Próvai (a pun on 'okay' in Irish and a slang term for the Provisional IRA) play themselves in the film (having taken acting lessons to prepare), the first two young Belfast natives and the third an older music teacher from Derry, the last associated more formally with the Northern Irish political movement for Irish language equality. The origin story of the band is presented as having this music teacher effectively 'discover' the two poetic rappers through the police translation encounter, thus joining together to form the band. The film imagines a lost dad of the two younger members, an IRA man played by Michael Fassbender, who is supposed to have faked his own death and now lives somewhere else under an assumed identity, teaching yoga and surfing to hippy tourists: 'from Bobby Sands to Bobby Sandals' (Peppiatt 2024). The band are depicted (by all accounts, a realistic portrayal) as vehemently refusing to confirm to ideological purism (this latter purity often associated with both the Irish language and Republican Nationalist movements in Ireland). One of the band has a covert relationship with a woman from a Protestant Unionist background, Georgia – their differences become a version of bedroom kink – and the trio are involved in supplying drugs in the high rises of West Belfast, with a hilarious portrayal of anti-drugs Republican thugs (*Radical Republicans Against Drugs* or *RRAD*). Both of these 'crimes' – fraternising with the purported 'enemy' and being involved in illicit or hedonistic activities – make the band a 'legitimate target' for punishment from the terror thugs, and the 'kneecap' scene is one of the highlights of the film. Again, and tragi-comically, much of this narrative is all too realistic for those of us who grew up watching daily updates on punishment beatings and worse on (Northern) Irish BBC and Ulster Television in the '70s and '80s.

From a Southern Irish perspective (where the native language is more spoken than in the North but still in a minority), the phrase 'Irish language movement' often signifies a traditional philosophical vision, of looking back. This is captured in the film when the characters talk about wanting to free the language from being a 'like the last Dodo, living behind glass in captivity....I want to smash the glass and set it free' (Peppiatt 2024). However, both North and South, there have also been significantly anti-traditional and progressive elements to the Irish language movement, which might be seen as forerunners of *Kneecap*'s more iconoclastic approach. For example, in Cork city in the early 1970s, a revolution in Irish-language poetry was about to be launched on the banks of the river Lee. The seminal inspiration for this emergent grouping was the artistic vision of Corkonian composer and musician Seán Ó Riada, while the existentialist Cork poet Seán Ó Ríordáin (Ó'Ríordáin 2014) kept a typically critical eye on proceedings. In this particular context, a group of four pioneering poets established a journal that would alter the course of Irish-language poetry and literature. This journal was called *Innti*. In a collection of essays, *Inside Innti. A new wave in Irish poetry* (Ni Gherabhuigh and Rosenstock 2023), recent Irish commentators and poets contextualise the significance of this progressive vision of

Irish language poetry in a manner that I think is prescient for the emergence of *Kneecap*'s poetics.

Kneecap's first album *Fine Art* (2024) involves a significant collaboration with Dublin post-punk band *Fontaines DC* in the shape of the song *Better Way to Live* which involves vocals from Fontaines lead singer Grian Chatten. *Fontaines DC* themselves have connection back to poetics and the relation between music and verse. The title of the band's debut album, *Dogrel* (2019) is a self-deprecating homage to 'Doggerel' the working-class 'poetry of the people' popularized by William McGonagall and the band have stated that they first bonded over a shared love of poetry. They also collectively released two collections of poetry – *Vroom* (inspired by American Beat poets) and *Wingding* (inspired by Irish poets) – before recording their debut album. Chatten is also a perceptive lyricist. Hailing from the Dublin North County seaside town of Skerries (himself the product of an Irish-English marriage), his songs foreground the overt but dark romanticism (as well as climate) of his home city (DC in the band name refers to Dublin City), as in the song *Big*'s 'Dublin in the rain is mine, a pregnant city with a Catholic mind'. Chatten also sings in a thick and heavy North Dublin brogue and his lyrics often connect to the national literary tradition, for example *Boys In The Better Land*'s shout out to another local and infamous muse; 'The radio is all about a runway model, with a face like sin and a heart like a James Joyce novel'.

Kneecap's Northern Irish 2024 album *Fine Art*, as a title and a concept, can similarly be seen as playing with the relation between art and the everyday, the beautiful and the ugly, the high and the low. 'Better Way to Live' itself lyrically foregrounds the existential quest to live a more meaningful existence (depicted in the film in the context of the Northern Irish Troubles). The song moves between the two languages of Irish and English with ease, a highly unusual feat in the context not only of popular music but even of literature. While most Irish writers (North and South) employ English as their chosen language of expression, a minority use Irish. But to employ both/and rather than either/or as a principle of expression and of poetics, and within the same text, is highly original and provocative.

For example, in the following verse, 'Faoi dheireadh tá deireadh tagtha le mo rut/Mar bhí lá maith agamsa inniu buíochas le foc/So I stroll I dtreo an pholl sa Bhalla/Four digit code, what do you know its Mo Chara' (Kneecap 2024). The four lines mix Irish and English wilfully and the aesthetic and semantic effect is surprisingly effective and immediate (whatever language(s) you speak). 'Finally my rut has ended/Because I had a good day today, thank fuck/So I stroll towards the hole in the wall/4 digit code, what do you know its My Friend'. By choosing this hybrid mix of languages, *Kneecap* enact a poetic pluralism, but also a political openness to the other. If it is true that 'gach focal a labhraítear i nGaeilge… is é piléar scaoilte ar son saoirse na hÉireann' (Every word of Irish spoken.. it is a bullet for Irish freedom), according to the character of the absent father Arló Ó Cairealláin in the film (*Kneecap* film 2024), then what is happening in the poetics of *Kneecap* is something different, a kind of *third space* beyond the old antagonism and dualism of English (Bearla) vs Irish (Gaeilge). It is not coincidental that this song also in its title points towards a different, but also a new and progressive form of existence for Northern and Southern Ireland – *Better Way to Live* (*Bealach Níos Fearr Chun Cónaí*).

We started with Robert Kelly's claim for Rothenberg that he played the role 'which Picasso played for the painters.. opening the sparkling world that comes when you crack open literature and see the primal gestures of oral energy and sudden imagery from which it all surges' (Kelly quoted in Rothenberg 2013). This conception of *a primal oral energy* from which literature derives has an especial relevance for the origins of Irish writing, as the Gaelic tradition is one which has a powerfully rich oral tradition of storytelling and of expression. It seems most appropriate then to be analysing the 'fine art' of a contemporary Irish Hip Hop poetics. Rothenberg evolved a central vision of what he came to call 'Deep Image'. Through this vision of experimental writing, he shakes up received ideas of what poems ought to be like. Poems can be everywhere, anything and everything, what he refers to as an 'omni-poetics' (Rothenberg 2013). In many respects, one can see both *Kneecap* and other poetic practitioners of contemporary music (such as *Fontaines DC*), as descendents of the earlier American counter-culture in this respect (Chatten especially refers back to the inspiration of the Beat poets and of Kerouac)[5].

In this manner, I see *Kneecap*'s Irish language Hip Hop (effectively punk) poetics, alongside the artistic vision of others such as *Fontaines DC*, as allies in the expressionistic new wave of transformation out of a hegemony of parasitism across much of contemporary arts and media. To this end, let me add a *haiku* dedicated to the subject of this essay (in a dual Gaeilge/English mode, up front and then translated).

Kneecap Haiku

You'll end up face down

In a back alley way

Unless you speak as Gaeilge

---

[5] This has inspired in my own work the development of a hybrid form full length book, including examples of metafiction and prose poems as well as verse, entitled *Deep Image* (Irwin 2025 forthcoming). In this extended text, I have sought to operationalise this philosophy of *l'écriture* (also with a tip of the beret to Jacques Derrida), juxtaposing metafiction texts with prose poems, haikus and shorter verse. In our times of contemporary crisis, it is hoped that the writing of poetry and of poetics, as a kind of *minor literature*, might serve and supplicate as a surprisingly robust resource *contra* the banality of mainstream culture (whether Spotify, Facebook or worse).

In a Hip Hop style

Tiocfaidh ár lá

Agus Georgia in lingerie

She's screaming the North

Belongs to the Brits

You're not convinced

But you'll agree 100%

With a Prod bird who

Gives the best head

Who wouldn't?

Anyway God is bust

Buíochas le foc

Plus a rhyming rap

That disses IRA

But just as much DUP

Leaving us laughing

Pissing féin

Loving our United Nations

Tráthnóna na teangan in Éirinn

Gach duine

A people once again

Kneecap Haiku (trans. English)

You'll end up face down

In a back alley way

Unless you speak [in Irish]

In a Hip Hop style

[Our day will come]

[And] Georgia in lingerie

She's screaming the North

Belongs to the Brits

You're not convinced

But you'll agree 100%

With a Prod bird who

Gives the best head

Who wouldn't?

Anyway God is bust

[Thanks be to fuck]

Plus a rhyming rap

That disses IRA

But just as much DUP

Leaving us laughing

Pissing ourselves

Loving our United Nations

[Late evening for language in Ireland]

[Every person]

A people once again

(Irwin 2025)

LA BEAUTÉ

EST DANS LA RUE

References

Bradshaw, Peter (2024) *Kneecap*. Film Review. The Guardian, Summer 2024.

Fontaines DC (2019) *Dogrel* (album). Partisan Records, London, UK.

Irwin, Jones (2025) *Deep Image*. Tofu Ink Press, California, US.

Kneecap (2024) *Fine Art* (album) Heavenly Records. London, UK.

Ni Gherabhuigh, Ailbhe and Rosenstock, Tristan (2023) *Inside Innti. A new wave in Irish poetry.* Cork University Press, Cork, Republic of Ireland.

Ó'Ríordáin, Seán (2014) *Rogha dánta* (Selected poems). Yale University Press, New Haven and London. Edited by Frank Sewell. Foreword by Paul Muldoon.

Peppiatt, Rich (Dir.) (2024) *Kneecap*. Film. Fine Point Films. Northern Ireland Screen's Irish Language Broadcast Fund and Screen Fund. Fís Éireann/Screen Ireland. Dublin and Belfast.

Rothenberg, Jerome (2013) *Eye Of Witness. A Jerome Rothenberg Reader.* Edited with Heriberto Yépes. Black Widow Press, Boston, MA, USA. 2013.

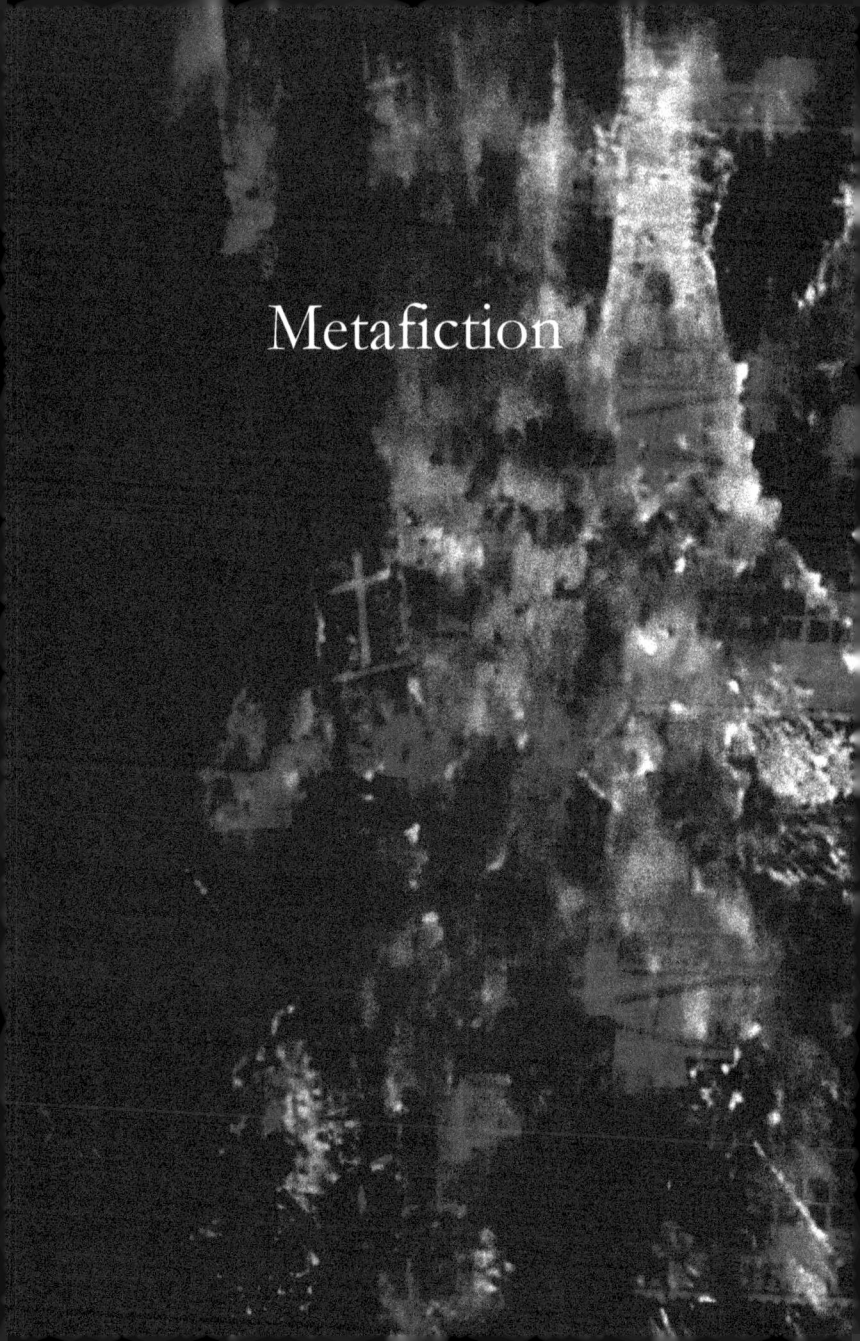

Metafiction

Who Killed Gilles Deleuze? Episode 1.

Twentieth century philosophy is fatalistically encumbered by its over—professionalisation. Life at the post-Kantian University is not amenable to risk and perturbance. It fosters a dry, measurable scholarly visage and frowns on Wild Beauty and Supernatural Interference. Of course, there are honorable exceptions to this bland contagion and these surrounds of Rationalist cranks.

First up, Ludwig Wittgenstein. His *Tractatus* is worthy of comparison to Duchamps in its conceptual Modernism and its sheer sense of philosophical daring. This man gives Analytic and Anglo-American philosophy a good name, as if Pollock had forgone Action Painting for the joys of minute and precious semantics. It took a foreigner to restore the sexiness of Oxbridge ordinary language and the everyday.

Second up, a man from France. Louis Althusser. Befuddled by May '68 and the incapacity of his obtuse economistic version of late Marx to say anything whatsoever about real life and real transformative revolutions happening outside his front window (as with most Marxists), he instead chose to make his life a Psychiatric Work of Art. Not before having grappled creatively with the whole psychoanalytic legacy, turning and twisting Freud and Lacan into shapes hitherto unrecognisable. Shame about his poor wife, though.

Last but not least, our bould Gilles. A man who handwrote all his books and got his long- suffering wife Fanny

(Grandjouan from Limousin) to type them up for Gallimard. She learnt her stylistics concerning hieroglyphic grammatology in Pierre Balmain's Parisian fashion house, no less. Let me suggest then a theory, unorthodox I grant you.

Shocked by what happened to Mrs. Althusser, and more than aware of the many illicit borrowings from vulgar Marxism and a poor man's Althusserianism (without the balls) in her husband's handwritten and oftentimes nearly illegible handscribbled meanderings, my hunch is quite simply that Fanny got in there first. She also felt that Gilles needed to pay handsomely for all the nasty asides about proto-feminism in such infamously overrated texts as *Anti-Oedipus*. Standing beside her wheezing asthmatic beau at the window of that 7th Floor apartment, she resolved that 7 floors was indeed a perfectly long (a suitably sufficient and just) distance to fall. Was it or was it not a rather putrid coincidence that the Deleuzes' apartment in the fifteenth *arrondissement* was just around the corner from the Police Lost and Found *and* the local Slaughterhouse.

Deleuze himself was most likely wise enough (despite the awful handwriting and cloying misogyny) to see this extraordinary Mariticide as precisely a condition of cultural emergence. He may have looked back at the last moment and decided to become complicit (I do not thereby suggest any prior knowledge on his part, just an instantaneous YES). Let's be honest. Some of his critics had already circled the wagons to call charge on a certain rather weak-willed voyeurism in his *oeuvre*. He would often retire to his study, having read these baneful reviews, and demonstrate a mood of hurt and immense fragility. Oh, how misunderstood am I, he would tell his cat, Felix, who appeared always unsurprised and unsympathetic. When you say that I am someone who's always just tagged along behind, taking it easy, capitalizing upon other people's experiments, on gays, on drug-users, alcoholics, masochists, lunatics, and so on, vaguely savouring their transports and poisons without ever taking any risks – frankly, I sob sob sob when I read these diatribes *contra-moi*, he would say to Felix, breaking out into uncontrollable snotty tears. These barbs undoubtedly cut poor Gilles up, even if they made his co-writer Guattari seem exactly the opposite and the real driver of the *whole avant-garde* endeavour. After all, wasn't Deleuze really only a fair to middling philosophy lecturer on the faculty at Vincennes, like a whole load of other ideologues (Badiou and Lyotard included, the former who hated Deleuze even more than the critics, often sabotaging his lectures with the help of Molotov cocktails and his Maoist terroristic students?) Guattari, on the contrary, was a man with a political mission, genuinely changing the psychiatric institution in France and beyond, as well as shaking the foundations of its social manifestations. Even the Maoists could see that Guattari was a worthy opponent.

Murder also (when done well, in an exemplary style) is capable of reaching the creative heights of a shocking poetics (say that of a heroin addicted Leopoldo Maria

Panero) and/or a novel that usurps grammar (say that of heterosexual-hating Katy Acker). In this weird zone of historical *coincidentia* of (seeming) minor accidents, predicted by the late Medieval eunuch De Cusa amongst others, one sees something emerge which is indeed truly bastardised by any conventional standards of decency, but also a kind of boon for the bohemian soul (currently struggling amidst the crass bureaucracy of late-late capitalist cybernetics).

Another final angle, dear reader. Our specific hero Fanny Grandjouan of Limousin's gesture, that rather dramatic push off the edge (dramatic for Fanny, usually a willing and subordinate typist) may have been precisely a faithful and paradoxical rendering, an ultimate eschatological realization, of her drasted hubby's Transcendental Materialist project. How so? Well can't we say that when it comes to EXPRESSION, that a less fashionable concept for late twentieth century European thought would be hard to find. For many years, for many schools of 'thought', expression has indeed been deeply anathema. The underlying assumption has been that expressionism can only amount to an uncritical subjectivism. But what if – AU CONTRAIRE – Fanny's deft hand was exactly the expression of a truly self-governing, reflective individual whose thwarted but superior inner life (all those foolish handscribbles, all those hours misspent in dictation) now emerged in the most aesthetic voluntary congregation of communication with the universe, here now in the moment of her bould Gilles' stumble, fall and final SPLASH on the ground down below.

Admittedly, there may be other hypotheses admissible. I can think of one at least, involving Durtal (or even J.K Huysmans himself), and a ritual that was performed in secrecy during the closure hours of the *Sûreté Générale*, the bureau of National Criminal Investigation. *Come, come. You surely don't believe that at this very moment, the Devil is being evoked and the Black Mass celebrated?* Just imagine that, a supernatural and Magick crime act instantiated on the very premises of the venerable detectives of the French Government (lying in abeyance for Gilles even in the years before his birth), incubated in the Underworld at this very acute moment of *fin-de-siècle* decadence.

Durtal knew all this (as in a kind of divine Satanic foreknowledge) the very first time he met the exquisitely evil Mme Chantelouve. She marched straight into his *Sûreté Générale* office, it was early May, late nineteenth century, and the weather was unusually humid, which drew out the emergent eroticism in a way that was wholly uncomfortable for our civil servant hero. He sat there frankly dumbfounded. What was he to do with the ardent entreaties that only had been communicated in secret letters heretofore? *If I love her*, he found himself saying aloud in her very presence, what kind of love can this be?

- What kind of distorted *eros* might we describe this to be, when all venerable and dignified *agathos* has thoroughly left the building, like a balloon that in a flash loses its air and whizzes around the room hauntingly and shrill? There is also, may I say, a rank and frightening esoteric fragrance (a rather romantic and unsuitable word for the phenomenon) now permeating our office environs. I don't think I speak exaggeratedly when I can call this current state of affairs at the *Sûreté Générale* as some kind of maleficent *possession.*

Not forgetting that no less a reader than Valèry had called aesthetic (and literary-political) attention to the very particular and strange intermingling of past and present in the character of Durtal and what he succeeded in operationalizing all around him. In a significant conceptualization, Valèry referred to this textual moment as a 'parallel demonstration'. If it is clear that this line of thought and flight of fancy is indeed parallel, we might ask however in what precisely constitutes its demonstration? At this point in time (and with a furtive look over our shoulder), we might protest that this paradigmatic question of questions is simply unanswerable. *If we want to keep our life, we might say.* The piece of evidence we had received in a wholly dissimulative manner (a coded missive worthy of Pynchon's postal service from *Inherent Vice*) that *there were suggestions that Deleuze had been visited in the middle of the night by a Stranger*, while an extraordinary progress in the case, also left us as interminably exposed and vulnerable. As someone known to be possibly 'in the secret know', we were now undoubtedly in mortal danger. Remembering in a crucial manner that to stay alive, to self-preserve, is also stay on the trail, to continue the role of Metaphysical Detective in this curiouser and curiouser mystery.

Not All Priests Are On The Side Of The Good

I

After a childhood haunted by the Other Side, surrounded by a set of Rationalist cranks who refused to accept the possibility of interference. Reader, I know different now let's call it *The Occult*. When confronted by Demons of whatever sort, best play it cool first avoid Angst. Not that's there nothing to be afraid of. Believe me, there is. Lots. But what? Spells, maybe to start. I knew a priest who Sunday Mass in the West of Ireland cursed a whole poor, terrified family off the pulpit and, within a week, a house fire burned them all out except the father who was blinded. That's 12 children and a mother. Ruthless and brutal. Ash. No forgiveness. No coincidence. Devils, they work with symbols and Not All Priests Are On The Side Of The Good.

What of it? The Manichean in me sees how it all fits together. Two personalities, two ontologies in One. Deleuze called it *Capitalist Schizophrenia* and he wasn't stupid or cowardly, although he did die by jumping from the 7th Floor. So, if there is some meaning you can find, better whisper it low then keep it secret. And try to survive. There were suggestions that Deleuze too had been visited in the middle of the night by a Stranger. The story fits. Guattari proclaimed pure innocence of course, as did Deleuze's philosophical adversaries although it was notable Badiou had no reasonable alibi to hand.

II

How to respond? Well, think up the possibility of being able to kill or otherwise harm someone by casting spells on them. That heavy, gilt framed mirror crashed to the ground at the very spot. Also, the room and its elements are prone to a surrounded sense of invisible, not always silent forces. All evening an anxiousness with unpleasant tactile sensation abounds. There are those who practice Black Magic each day before supper and Eduoard Dubus, that young poet responsible for propelling the table round Berthe de Courrière's apartment, is a paradigmatic example. All my life I have been followed by voices, have joined Occultic circles. I am said to be extremely high-strung, naively credulous. But I can assure you of this; the Devil exists and the power He enjoyed in the Middle Ages has not been taken from him. Read St Augustine of Hippo's voluminous writings and you will see this prophecy starkly enunciated, between the lines obliquely. In *The City of God* most especially, awaiting the Vandals, there is that fatalistic creeping Dread, Augustine almost ready to admit that the whole thing has been scripted from the beginning of the beginning.

III

Take note of the rumour concerning Durtal, that modern anti-hero Counter-Enlightenment man. Was he agonized or alienated in any genuine way or was it just Angst employed as an occultic nay aesthetic ruse? Oh, *I am so robbed of religion and plunged into decadence by the pressures of modern life*, says Durtal oh so exhibitionistically, with his beloved, very own self-same Persecution Complex, but he fails to look into our eyes directly and has that furtive askance stare of a man with a secret agenda. As if he doesn't mean it and perhaps never did. Could he really be faking it, dear reader? For the sake of literature, say.

He has discovered a new Road to Rome. God's Death, the hyperbolic death of the monotheistic one true Deity, is but a temporary disappointment for Durtal. A slight hiccup. Of course, this nonchalance of the bould Durtal draws down on him, on his very corporeal and mortal body, the moralistic wrath of the Catholic Church who convict our modern anti-hero of the obscene crime of obscenity. But, all things considered, isn't it that precise denunciation and estrangement from the pathways of the Moral and Good Life, to become one of the Damned of the Earth, isn't it that specific morbid fate which constitutes exactly our anti-hero Durtal's most treasured Dream of Ultimate Exile? Woe upon woe, how can one such human, born amongst us fragile and weak beings, be both so vain and so admirable at the very same time? *Paradox*. Although a tendency to paradox was hardly the worst of his weaknesses, or of his strengths.

There is another story told that having conjured up this extraordinary figure in the languid afternoons of the French Civil Service bureau of the Ministry of the Interior, his disregarding author J.K. Huysmans had decided that this line of thought just wouldn't cut it in the *fin-de-Siècle* aesthetic world and that he would have to go back to the writing board. Realising the dangers associated with meddling in this way with occultic characters, Huysmans had taken every precaution, from visiting a Witch Doctor to consulting his psychiatrist, as well as re-reading the memoirs of the infamous Gilles De Rais. Taking account of as much of this advice as was possible in the circumstances, our bold author resolved to burn the relevant pages of his extant manuscripts in a midnight pyre one October night, so as to finally banish this wretched cur of the imagination from the purviews of humanity. Not simply the passages where Durtal featured overtly but also any secondary suggestion of his involvement or even of his existence, and even finally any line of the extant text which seemed to carry in its direction the potential of leading to the emergence of such a villainous anti-hero, would have to be excommunicated and banned from utterance or from memory forthwith. Alas, the fateful October night was, as if by chance, one where the wind blew down from the North through the skies of Paris and before Huysmans could intervene, much of the pyre's materials seemed to take off in a hallucinatory release of wild pages, which, as they rose in a concentric circle into the dark skies to depart this scene, appeared to mark out their very lines one by one, mocking their now distraught author, who could only dear reader, now fear the Absolute Worst.

That Summer Feeling

Do you remember that summer feeling? C'mon reader, *think*. Way back in the days and evenings before 2020, we often used to bask in the glory of an anticipated run of consistent and unadulterated joying (or *jouissance* as the French rather more rudely put it) from late May through to the end of August. Even in early September as the days shortened, you could still often reap the rewards of a lazy, hazy holiday *soujourn* and even the adult return to work and the children's kickback to school seemed like an extension of relative freedom (especially if you could afford an Autumnal siesta now and again).

I remember, in the acute anticipation of this sensibility's imminent arrival, being in a café queue in later Springtime and I'm trying to explain to some people I've never ever met even once before about that certain, specific yet somehow elusive feeling. 'It's That Summer Feeling', I say, trying to indicate what it is about the hazy sunlight shining through the shop window which is making people widely smile and jive around a bit curiously from left to right. I mean the song but I can see that one of this small grouping, a woman in her early 30s tall with gothic earrings and wearing all over black, has misunderstood me to be talking just generally about an existential feeling that humans might experience any given day, but especially today. This small group of two women and one man, in the queue just ahead of me, have undoubtedly already succumbed to this extraordinary charm of the season as they are ordering some incredibly sunny conglomeration of *frappuccinos* which has the *baristas* in a bit of a tizz. As practice makes perfect and, up until now, the demand for these new-fangled caffeine concoctions has been lying significantly dormant on a door-to-door level.

Thankfully, Maria behind the big *formica* counter, who is from Croatia and who has a distinctly resilient character, takes over from Alex who is from Sicily and who has a predilection (much as I count him as one of my all-time fave *baristas*; top 5 unequivocally although not higher than say number 4) for dizziness and lack of efficiency under pressure. The art of coffee making under late, late capitalism in the weary but nonetheless restless West of Europe has emerged as a hybrid mix of the aesthetic and the economic, but as the latter variable has become more dominant in the industry the remaining aesthetes in the profession (a diminishing breed, no doubt) can often come under undue moral pressure from the incessant norms of Neoliberal hyper-productivity output. Maria, with her own undoubted and authentic aesthetic dimension inherited from the 1970s Zagreb underground of which her father was a noted luminary, nonetheless has learned to balance this with neo-industrial surface conformism. Alex, about 24, 6ft 2, bearded and big boned, is a more independent spirit and, let's say, *not* a good listener when it comes to the Boss, or more generally the Man. More power to him, I say, this Italian Stallion (as he is known by all the local girls who frequent this particular establishment in unusually large and frenetically hormonal numbers). That said, Leftist ideology notwithstanding (his grandmother spent time in a prison with Antonio Gramsci for union activities in one of the radicalised Fiat car plants and could recite the *Prison Notebooks* by passage), his abrasive if admirable personal politics are noticeably holding up the bloomin' queue. It now stretches as far as the *Oscar Wilde Barbers* on the town centre diamond. We better be careful or that effusive, seemingly unconditional high we all are experiencing might get taken away again. Not quite yet, though, as Maria salvages the moment and gets the icy numbers concocted and delivered to these three eager consumers sooner than any of them can say General Tito or Non-Alignment Pact back at her.

All is well with our little world again, thankfully and I am full of gratitude, as if I were nearly some kind of Christian. 'It's That Summer Feeling', I say. I mean the song but as the gothic girl (and probably her two friends as well) have misunderstood me to mean a universal emotion of humanity, there is no point in me quoting the lyrics then to explain as that might further compound the confusion, but I do anyway, as I can't think of anything better to say myself.

So off I go mock-singing 'When there's things to do not because you gotta, When you run for love not because you oughta', and I can now unequivocally see that this woman is impressed with me because she thinks I'm some kind of spontaneous poet who is able to put such complex, singular feelings of humanity not just into words but into words that rhyme. What a man, what a poetic SuperHero.

And yes, don't get me wrong, I am delighted that this has happened, it's fantastic, it's a flippin' good thing. But I can't help feeling guilty that the only way I've managed to impress this undoubtedly attractive woman, as well as her purely innocent and somewhat naïve compatriots, is by deceiving her regarding the originality of my material on feelings and their relation to brightness and to the wider world. Also, I don't think the great American proto-punk lyricist and seer Jonathan Richman (considered by many to be, with his band *The Heartbreakers*, the unique segueway between the high Sixties of the *Velvet Underground* and the low Seventies early Punk) would be too pleased with this kind of, well let's speak honestly, *this kind of plagiarism*. After all, didn't both of these phases of modern popular music, for all their particularity, nonetheless share a rather rabid emphasis on the value of originality and original creativity of the artist *ex nihilo* as their unnegotiable values basis and their *sine qua non*?

Interview with Dennis Cooper

'Wish that I could eat your cancer when you turn black'
Cobain

i

A way of talking about things, Cooper had a way of talking
about things. One subject would flow into another but not
effortlessly. Abrasion was his middle name, in all things,
actions as well as his speaking voice and cognitive thread,
and of course his very appearance. He was unabashedly
queer growing up, from as soon as I can remember and
although I don't have a great memory, still that's a long time
ago. When I say unabashedly, it sounds like he wasn't trying
to hide it but it was more than that really. It was clear in his
tonality of voice, a little lighter and more languid, somehow
more intimate for a man, he was softer but also lascivious so
he made you feel that his voice was undressing you and
sizing you up but slowly and never as a come-on. This was
intellectual eroticism, more as a sense of homosexual
understanding, where you rated on his lifeworld's compass,
North South East or West, and how you registered, fuckable
or lovable or neither. Understood from a purely
epistemological perspective you understand, albeit it was still
a kind of objectification. Maybe sometimes, rarely, you might
rate both for Cooper, that is fuckable and lovable
epistemologically and simultaneously. I was certainly fuckable
but I don't think he could ever love me. And him for me?
Well, I never entertained any real feelings of fuckability when
it came to Cooper. Sure, I'll admit, I did like his style, the way
he looked and moved and had his being. Then again, who
didn't?

Studying Cooper was not an exact science. But you can start with the physicals, which contain less ambiguity. He had the longest and most sensitive hands that I've ever seen and his fingers were bony aesthetic, as if they were expensive antiques or the stone figures of an ancient Athenian statue masquerading as digits for everyday use. His long blonde hair was almost like a girl's or that of a marine goddess, the way it twirled and spun around in tight curls, the way it would fly out in all directions when he ran or jumped or played guitar, the way he would flick his neck to draw attention to his gorgeous mane. His lips were thick and ruby full, always pursing in a mock pout when he would address a serious topic, and he rarely wasted time on the superficialities of existence. No ordinary man, then. He knew it well too, of course. His favourite phrase being *it ain't my fault I keep turning you on*. What do you say to that?

ii

Some writers and artists are harder to track down than others. Hubris gets in the way or maybe they're just insanely busy on some new project. With Cooper he ran a famous and controversial blog (finally excommunicated from the internet) and made himself available to his readers, so all I had to do was send an email. I had a reply in days.

Yes Mr Tim Dlugos, sure thing I remember us growing up together. I'd be delighted to talk to you, just send on some questions in advance, we can generally stick to that rubric but let's leave some room for some organic and spontaneous play. To be honest, I'm flattered that you want to discuss my work which isn't false modesty but I'm always a little surprised when people get what I'm trying to do. Of course, I often inspire exactly the totally opposite reaction, especially recently and I

have a thick skin so it doesn't kill me or make me want to kill me, but
lately yeah I have been a bit low about the constant flak. You're
probably following the Google trouble, fucking corporate cocksuckers.
So, let me confirm; flattered. Happy to know you, Mister Dlugos, again
after all these bloomin' years man.

Wow, Dennis Cooper was flattered by little old me. Sure, I was excited.

I thought up some what I at least thought were pertinent questions, which didn't take me that long, truth be told, as I was somewhat of a Cooper obsessive. Of course, I don't necessarily say that proudly. After all, Cooper's paradigmatic themes of death, abusive relationships and the search for language to convey extreme emotions may say something about the character of their author, but they also tell something about the fragmented *psyche* of the readers drawn to his work. Maybe due to our shared background, Dennis and I could blame the environment, eh?

But looking around the café we are meant to meet I'm thinking everyone is a bit fragmented these days. I'm sitting at a table in *The Onyx*, a dimly lit east Hollywood coffeehouse and sure this is well middle-class bourgeois but you can see the hustlers outside on the sidewalk, scoring and jonesing.

That's Dennis storming through the entrance. For some reason he reminds me of Lee Majors when he played *The Million Dollar Man*. I think about saying this when he arrives at my table (I have waved so he recognises me although I'd also sent a cute pic through the email) but decide against it. Thing is, I don't remember ever Cooper talking about the rehabilitation of 1970s American machismo idols, not the heterosexist ones that is. So, I keep schtum. I've resolved anyhows to stick to more intra-literary questions and mostly about his own work, as let's face it I'm a fan. That's why I'm here. And looking at my watch somewhat nervously, it's already fifteen minutes past midday and he did say he had another appointment at 2. Also, we need to order. Lordy, the stress! Honestly, I would not want to be doing this every day.

Still, I wasn't gonna waste the gilded opportunity after all this time now was I? Truth be told, there were demons from the past that needed finally to be put to bed. Course Cooper knew this as well as I did.

So, Tim, what's this meeting really about, I mean, what's it really about then?

Shit, man.

I thought this latter phrase to myself although a seer like Cooper could undoubtedly read the script off my silent lips.

Where to hide, now?

After the Death of God - A Fictional Biography of Dissident Surrealist Georges Bataille

Preface

So, you think you know what's what? Well, sorry to say, no you don't. Life and existence are a process of intensive and deepening ambiguation. This happens primarily through just being there in so-called real time but if you are prone or sensitive to literature then the derangement of the senses is rather acute. The activity of 'l'écriture' or writing is only one of the most beautiful of these disorientations alongside love, sex, death and all things philosophical. Writing subjects everything to a process of 'glissement' or sliding. There is no cure, there is no redemption. The fictional biography of Georges Bataille is one of our most paradigmatic examples.

Episode 1

'with the positing of the individual, the Beyond is established' Hegel, 1807.

One imagines Bataille in a *bordello*, maybe one of the ones he regularly frequented in Pigalle, late 1930s. He is trying to explain to one of the hostesses how everything can only be understood not simply in terms of the death of god, but in terms of atheology.

- My dear Lydia, atheology is not atheism. Not in the slightest. This is where drasted Sartre has me all wrong.

- Ah, yes, *peut-être*. Poor Jean-Paul was here just last week and indeed I found him very confused. Also, how can an existentialist be so goddamned ugly?

- Ah my dear Lydia, I find you utterly enticing as well as metaphysically astute. Bravo!

- Very well Georges, I accept your compliments with gratitude. Of course, I recognise you as the only authentic Lord of Excess, making all the false suitors pale into the background.

Thus did Bataille thoroughly earn his reputation, mixing high theory and low practice in a demonic hybrid unequalled then or now. But Georges wasn't yet finished as, although hardly suffering from false modesty, nonetheless he considered the admiration of his beloved Lydia only worthwhile if properly deserved. As a true metaphysician of the Dark, and a purported inheritor of the Symbolist legacy and mantle, he was conscious of the need for the recognition of excess to be justified by a thoroughgoing atheology. Also, in accordance with the old Heraclitean principle of opposites *meet* (stolen and passed off as original philosophics by the bastard Christian medievalist eunuch known as de Cusa), such syllogistic logic must also be rendered accessible in a *bordello*. From high to *bordello*, from *bordello* to high. Otherwise, frankly, null and void. Otherwise, truly, not worth the naked skin they are written on, such logicisms. In this, we follow the bould Hegel who was a lot madder and less rational than the traditionalists suppose.

- Dear Lydia, while indeed grateful to you for your kind words, I have one further task in hand before we might descend to the dungeon of whips.

- Oh, Georges, don't delay as every second counts – also, every second costs and I know you have ill-spent most of your monthly Library salary even since last week.

- True, alas Lydia, you are right. But metaphysical syllogism bearing on abstract truth simply cannot wait, money or no money. As a true philosopher (as with Diogenes, aka *Socrates gone mad*!), I am willing to pay the full penalty. Perhaps, nonetheless, you can consider a perverse pedagogue's discount? Either way, let me make haste on my proof. You see, all these atheists such as Jean-Paul have got it wrong, arse-ways I tell you. They read Nietzsche's *Gay Science* and think that when he tells us that 'God is dead' that somehow this is intended as a defence of secular reason against divine superstition. But Lydia, my beautiful darling (oh how those deep brown eyes of yours seduce me so intensely and that V shape of yours where all of me is lost in unholy succor!), it is the very opposite that is true.   As my great confidante Pierre Klossowski (the brother of Balthus no less!, so we have it on aristocratic artist authority) succinctly rendered this fundamental if shocking truth; *the death of God does not culminate in an atheism, it continues rather.* Or in other words, the death of God may kill off the mothball theology (to which I say – good riddance! – although I remain fond of St Augustine's self-contortions) BUT it only frees up, in this very demise, the rest of our love and pain and sex and tears. And not just ours – but that repressed excess of the very WHOLE of the cosmos. I call this, dear Lydia, the liberation of *the Accursed Share*!

- Oh Georges, you are so much more handsome and sexy than Jean-Paul. I think I get most of what you are saying, though I may have got a bit lost there near the end. You do so speak as if in a kind of magical trance and it carries me away to far off terrains way beyond Pigalle, Monsieur Bataille. But alas, I have to remind you – time is money!

- Ah yes, you are of course (as always!) correct. Enough of the *Accursed Share* in the abstract. Let us descend to the dungeon where we may indeed (as if by magic) conjure up the materialisation of such metaphysical truths. To the cave we must go, Mistress, let us be patient no longer. [As an aside] By the way, did you remember to buy those pills for me?

- Of course, Master Georges, I am always completely attentive to your demands [laughs affectionately].

- Ah, Lydia, God may be dead, but you are indeed my Saviour and the only one worth having, are you not?

[the two descend down the stairs to the dungeon's semi-darkness, maintaining this heartfelt irreligiosity].

Prose and Longer Poems

Psychogeography

I

left to rot for untold years

The 16A goes to Keresley

But there is some kerfuffle

By the jewellers with a skateboard and a passerby's head

And once more there is blood on the Burges

And you would need all the pure water

In the putrid river Sherbourne

Running under Kong and the dented cans of alcohol

To clean up after the five fast food outlets

Including the newly extended McDonalds

An embarrassment to the city

Said a dishevelled Coventry councillor

Which is a pity for the Pay Day Loan shop

The Pawnbrokers the Casino the five Bookmakers

And the pre-war Cross

Which still gets a good soldier footfall

Almost as good as the now defunct Pink Parrot

And the VIP Cleopatra's

Not forgetting the pissing on themselves pensioners

On the mobility scooters after a few beers

Especially after a few beers

left to rot for untold years

And the bootboys are jeering

The Fire Brigade fleet

Who first came up the so-called no-go

At Ironmonger Row

And then drove the wrong way

Down the one-way road at Trinity Street

Obviously, they weren't thinking straight

Coming under undue pressure

Harry Finch, one of the store managers

Who works there

Says that *sometimes you look down here*

And it's quite intimidating

left to rot for untold years

II

Cast the city in concrete

Culvert the river

1960s boom no room

For nurture or nature

Cup your ears

By Cross Cheaping

And you'll hear

The slow flow Sherbourne

Gurgling towards Far Gosford street

The Ring Road is no longer safe

There is an Anarchist clerk in the Herbert Read

Who is planning an uncovering

Flood the mainland

A guerrilla outfit of Sherbourne settlers

Are worn from dry thirst

They fish and drink

Amidst the bins and back doors of murk

But the Sherbourne settlers will return

And with the neo-Syndicalist Herbert Read man

Will lead the whole of red-light Hillfields

And those still surviving in Wood End

In a big roadworthy boat

Down Palmer's Lane

To the original town of Cune

In the spirit of Mikhail Bakunin

Where the first bridges can re-emerge

And even the nonrevolving restaurant

In the old Precinct

Will stand on its head and dance

In a torn Punk t-shirt and fishnets

Serving amphetamine refreshment

To the resurrecting sounds of *Subway Sect*

And the romantic urban poetics of Vic Godard

Who we all thought was dead

But he ain't yet thankfully

Just like a confounding Christ

Once more our river run

Drink up jack up

Our reservoir rain

We are again drunk

Now is our time to STRIKE!

III

In the fields of Hawkes End

There is a clear stream

Which has been calling my name

Umpteen times in crisis

It was almost dry

Until I forced myself to cry

Bucketing the tears

Praying through my cupped Psalms

To get it up and running

Took me untold years

In 1941, the worst era

When the *Luftwaffe* were eerily spot on

We all nearly died – I kid you not! -

But somehow we survived

Never denying our religion

We are still here flowing

Heading south to the Sowe

Despite our crises

we stay low quay

IV

All is obviously not well

In Swanswell

As a man

Described as a Polish exile

Last seen leaving a brothel

About 5ft 7in tall

White, medium build

With a short black ball of hair

Heading towards Cox Street

In the city centre

Is no more

And earlier

There were

Lots of unverified rumours

Lots of racist murmurs

Lots of police cars

Ambulances and Fire Lorries

Lots of Right-Wing skins

Out at Swanswell

Which is the last bit of water

The only survivor after Pool Meadow

Which once upon a year

Was much larger

Part of a river

Before the final culver

Is now a West Midlands Bus server

So, all is not well

And the Polish exile

Who has been missing

For quite a while

Looks like he may have been killed

At Swanswell

Which joined with Pool Meadow

Was long ago

Part of Mill Dam

And once more

The disappeared river

May hold its horror

the immersed Sherbourne our tears

our murderous ancestors

drowning we surmise our Polish brother

V

As an emigrant also I too came originally

To this place much maligned

For being sent to

This place flattened by the *Luftwaffe*

Just like that

Which is just it – to be lost so fast

Brings insight

In short

I ended up happy to be

Sent right here nowhere else

Could compare

In this city, summer

Days mixed in with worn grey concrete

Some fight with guys or

Girls listening on Ghetto Blasters to

Ska. When Amy played *You're Wondering Now*

At Glastonbury with Terry Hall *et al* I nearly

Cried with joy. Scratch that, I *did* cry.

Dammers won't reform for whatever

Reason. You can throw the book at

Him but his father was a Protestant preacher

So instead put your hands together Amy

Is dead now so no matter. *Gangsters*

All these years later still

Sounds great. Pork-pie hats

And second-hand suits. I remember

A Derek Raymond *noir*

Set in the Two-Tone era

Where the guy grills the

Girl for supper. That's

What I call

Literature, buddy.

Never too happy to

Be here. The band

Couldn't stand each other but

That's just a mirror to society. Terry

Hall seemed always cranky

Enough. In Edenmore, we liked
That. In Coventry, we liked that
Even more. By the Pool Hall after
School. My favourite
Graffiti was the Bob Marley
Album cover *Exodus*. There was
Only one black face
Back in Edenmore. He took shit
But it wasn't racist. *Promise.*
Scratch that. *It was.*

Of Western Civilisation

Sweet and juicy criminality they said as if the fellas were
some wreckers of Western civilization when yeah maybe
they were seeking that but let's face it takes a lot more than a
couple of songs a fair bit of sneering and a few broken
hearts to change Big History so *what's love got to do with it* she
asked that first night wasn't just him then she was in fact the
one discouraging the use of condoms and undue affection
*don't do drama y'see I'm in it for the pleasure me w*hich took him a
little by surprise only by a little though cos Mark was hardly a
romantic post-romantic rather like Debord Vaneigem and all
that '68 mess where nothing gets cleaned in the revolution
just left totally ubiquitous filthy after a while the use of
amphetamine affects personal and mental hygiene for the
worse that said has its own sweet and juicy aesthetic War
brings circumstances with it that changes our normal
concepts of morality it's a tough dirty business caused in the
first instance by the filth of corruption so that's how it
started with a lustful kiss and little else fine they both
thought that's all there is best foundation for a revolution
War brings circumstances with it that changes our normal
concepts of morality it's a tough dirty business caused in the
first instance by the filth of corruption start with an end to
naivety look at reality full on face no Botox tricks please if I
show you ME and you show me YOU next let's get the
Semtex and the cheapest bomb making equipment on the
market War brings circumstances with it that changes our
normal concepts of morality it's a tough dirty business
caused in the first instance by the filth of corruption you
track the ones you want to hit day after day for a bit Belfast
you build up the record Bangor family train trips out by the
coast check the transport routes the times the acquaintances
the weak links not an exact science but with diligence you

can make progress just make sure you're not being watched
by police or informers trust the tiniest sub-set of breathers
simple soon the courage rises and the desire fix the date no
going back we are in this together War brings circumstances
with it that changes our normal concepts of morality it's a
tough dirty business caused in the first instance by the filth
of corruption so scratch that note earlier it *is* a kind of love
a special typology not everyone could do just this or just do
this n art of some sort helps to have chill in the blood as bad
a childhood as you can possibly muster a degree in the social
sciences above average 2:1 but not capable of First wrote
very well but somewhat dogmatic ultimate lack of feeling the
report from the state psychiatrist put it marked down for
that who died not long after in a mysterious and rather brutal
accident funny that

What Will Happen Then?

I

Behold! On this
island of Gods
I spied Dionysus
in a pair of speedos.

There he was
at the edge of rock
where Skala comes to meet Poros
writing a book.

It was a short text
to the scabrous point
written in squid ink
with a cover of Kephalonian pine.

What are you saying, O Dionysus,
I asked this old God, trying not to laugh
at his ridiculously fitting speedos,
in this long-awaited manuscript of yours?
At Poros, he replied oh-so-seriously,

I can only wish
that after the bloody Christians
and even the mimetic Moderns
have tried to suppress our stupendous Mystery,
that we cast out our unforgiving nets
once again for the long-lost fish.

II

When there weren't
enough fish and the
earthquake came
this became an island
of priests and the most
beautiful women in all Greece.

Nay! In the total Mediterranean.

Unhappy island then
of unfit husbands
and suffering sirens.
They wail at noon
like the Hellene Ferry

that leaves for Kyllini.

How I loved Artemis
until she tore me to pieces.

How I adored Athene
until she blinded me.

III

The man with the chairs
in the van red dark
with dirt and sand. In
his fifties swarthy with a
Kephalonian voice and a harsh
smile for a world gone nuts.

Barmy summer, he said,
with Brexit and bad
weather. Not as many
chairs required daily.

It's a niche market, he said.

The man with the chairs
in the dark red van.
Hoping for a better Autumn.

IV

Under the bigger stones
smooth the smaller ones
sharper on the soles which

move very slowly as everything
else here. The drop in
the early water is deep and
you fall into the azure

waves. Not far out is
a skerry you can clamber up
to pool the smaller
fish. I wonder if
the Fascists took time to
play here? I wonder if
you can find a change
of mind in an environment?

I wonder if

the post-rational world returns?

What will happen then?

V

Watch out for the New Right Wave

on the pebbled beaches of Kephalonia

when you lose your footing

half-naked. Not suave

you are a nervous swimmer.

The local boys laugh

your white skin an eye sore

even for the Right-Wingers.

The Levante Ferry has

a curious backwards

manoeuvre as it enters

Poros like Thrasymachus

when his 'might is right'

runs up against the *elenchus*.

Less might more flight from
philosophia although what
is moral defeat for a tyrant
eulogiser? *Just waiting, Socrates,*
for the Führer [now on perennial request],
whether me or someone even greater.

VI

As Cephalus
passed the question of justice
to his son Polemarchus,

so too Plato
passes the question of justice
to us.

Today, Saturday, at Poros,
I am struck only by this -
the question of justice *is*
the question of malice.

Also an inheritance
from Plato.
That the world is
as hard as it is.
Get with it.

VII

I saw the old Greek
guy fall from grace
where the sea meets
the stones on the
beach across the street Ithakos.

He holds up a mirror
to all us pro-Communists.

Be careful you get
the right swim shoes
or risk the Blues.

This Italian May

After Pasolini

I

A sultry haze rises

Across the Fish Market

Stalls mid-morning

If the sun can be

Enjoyed or feared

Here it is both

Dreams of unseen depths

Weary awnings

Beg to differ

II

The olive vendor sleeps

In a small whitewashed

Windowless shack that

Has curtains for doors

Friends with the ragman

Coming from some other

Slum they are

On intimate terms

Both keep a dusty

Merchandise that looks

Like stolen goods

And their cruelty

Increases the hardness

Of their faces

As their hunger

III

Catania, your uneven squares

Make me dizzy

But I too would like

To avoid earthquakes

Not always lucky

In this regard

An earthquake or two

Between friends

May of course be welcomed

But in my future

I will walk with a tilt

So as to avoid my worst fate

IV

As in a film by Pasolini it

Is early afternoon down

By the city's main bridge

Several youths strip to

Their waists and hurl

Themselves in with abandon

In this moment, there is peace

In the refusal of constraint

Later, at the Fish Market

A fist fight breaks out

In the three o'clock heat

There is peace in this also

In the humanity of gratuitous revolt

V

The light motorbikes

Make a dinny whir

Turning into the cobbled

Narrow streets of Catania's

Old Town the worn

Brakes screeching as if

In conversation with each

Other as us humans

Listen on intently

Desperate for clues to

Life's oblique mysteries

VI

To transfigure

Is to organise

For our goal

Is not just beauty

Though beauty

Is also a vision

In this case it

Keeps finding itself

In unusual places

Amongst different peoples

So, beautiful ones

Let us be judged by examples

And by our struggles

VII

These ancient walls

Throb again this near-summer

With Banksy slogans and

The blinding sunlight suggests

We must start again and that

Ex nihilo there is a hope

That a life collapsed in ruins

Is also a *tabula rasa*

Young man, in this Italian

May which now rises

Up with the historical dust

Of the historical past and

Makes you choke write anew

On the walls with a scrawl

That draws a fragile future

On illuminated concrete

Moira

Let me tell that tragi-comic tale once more the fast-talking
shower of queers no words just desires and drives wasn't
Moira the queen of them gangsters worser she was they said
especially in that King-sized bed of hers through the long
bleak Seventies she kept a feral house of strays had no qualm
with seeing a few slip away if necessary wasn't she meant to
have popped old Grisly Irish Raymond with her very own
hands they say she finished him with a claw hammer bashed
his ugly brains out all over the bar table the commotion
spilling the gang's collection of beer into the interstitial space
of O'Hara's exposed frontal lobes looked like a Pollock or
worser a Freud Francis Bacon laughed in the *Coach and Horses*
after in between gin Martini pints this bunch of neo-Action
Painters making startling order out of supposed chaos in
Soho even if to the untrained a mess nothing boring
anyhows ain't that right gangsters are sure vivid Moira loved
it lapped it up the minutes and the bloody seconds of evil
excitement their trembling fear her power her pleasure
getting her sexy long stockinged legs over the prettier Eton
Harries that chunky long leopard skin coat as a signature no
years in domestic hell or the clink for her myriad extortion
or murder cases taken out well before they got anywhere
near somewhere like court crooked cops death's sister
suppose you could file her under *sociopath* going way beyond
the individual with her set of intersubjective cronies a whole
Middlesex mini universe of cut-throat this and that hard
against the loftier values sown into the fabric of post-War

life iconoclast then though not sure she or hers stand for anything or if there was an underlying project of any kind other than greed and mayhem from the very get-go probably kicked-off with that Clacton-On-Sea heist which went badly wrong and they had to finish the bravely resistant postmistress who had already seen too much now we have all seen way too much but these days there can be no going back flashing her bristols was Moira *do you ever wonder* she asked *where the bodies go* the liquid slap of the head as they died one last oh soundful so sorrowful sigh that incongruous stare without any care not even looking over her shoulder I tryin' hard shoot elsewhere suggested the countryside anyhows I'd been thinking more about the souls after death like *out somewhere in the sticks nah fool boy*, she said, *not there where then* her bristols all pricked up now like she was gettin' extra-excited in her deep V you were lost you could well see she had plenty of what it took *really don't knows where why does it matter nowhere maybe* she laughs w*here's that baby* that hot red lipstick made her lips Satanic nowhere did exist I had been there years before I remembered dark place more sweaty than rock n' roll fever music deeper and scarier she was biting the quiver on her lower lip now *wanna be lovers* she asked *Moira* I said *yea sure* worst decision ever woman means you no harm her other boyos had said a soft spot there not to be believed could show you the snuff video tapes if I was allowed to keep 'em lucky to be still alive only cos I kept my mouth shut pusface plus eyes past is no window only a painting you gotta interpret or last night's performance you gotta forget I was never very good at sleeping soundly or at understanding pure malice weak me eh so off you go East London mate out towards Plaistow so as to read the concrete prose biblical there you can read the graffiti smells like piss at least it's real at least it is real like evil carnal learn your life lesson then move on if you possibly can then again maybe trouble never wants to move on maybe you cannot highlight the survivor bit won't let yourself remember Gisèle that woman what happened her hate has its reasons also Laima from Lithuania not Vilnius but Kaunas the smaller second city some faces you cannot ever forget disappeared one night by Moira and by her men we all knew the worst kind of slowly delayed end that one gave me running nightmares pregnant remains on a bonfire what could we do didn't find out until after of course 'wise intervened

Haikus and Shorter Poems

My Hands Are A City

My hands are a city, say Thessaloniki

They caress my burning face in the afternoon blaze

Yesterday was 34 today is even hotter

On the public bus we are all intimates

My hands reach out to an old man who is weeping

My hands cup his tears like a chalice

He says *efcharisto* but his lament is continuous

Compositional Note

I often write poems to the rhythm of my various modes of transportation day-to-day (running, walking, driving, trains, planes) that surreptitiously awaken my creative sense. Shorter poems are especially suited to this more instantaneous writing and, in recent years, I have taken a critical interest in how the *haiku* form of poem (with the strict three line and seventeen syllable count) was metamorphosed by Jack Kerouac under his conception of 'American Haikus'. The three-line original constraint became more fluid and dexterous. By loosening the line stricture of the traditional haiku, while keeping its sense of compression and meditative simplicity, the form affords new possibilities for grappling with the urban (and neo-rural) kaleidoscope, the whole maddeningly beautiful sometimes ghastly 'Open Field' which Charles Olson designated as the paradigmatic break between modernist and postmodernist poetics.

This was my catalyst for the opening line 'My hands are a city'. As a phrase, it is borrowed from (alongside Kerouac) Beat poet Gregory Corso's titled poem[6]. We can talk about *a philosophy of hands*. Our hands have a unique ability to touch, to explore, and to communicate, connecting us to our bodies, to others and to the surrounding environment. The

---

[6] The Beats are often underestimated as theorists of poetry, to the extent that their poetics is deliberately low-key or off-hand, effortlessly cool and urbane. This masks, to my mind, a greater complexity in their thought. Corso's poem 'My Hands Are A City' appears first in his collection *The Vestal Lady On Brattle*; 'My hands are a city, a lyre/And my hands are afire/And my mother plays Corelli, while my hands burn' (Corso, in TVLOB, included in *Gasoline*, City Lights, San Francisco, US, 1958).

French philosopher Jacques Derrida writes of our hands as 'meaning-making', something specifically human and humane (but also capable of perversion and of cruelty). Our hands enact our being-in-the-world, interfacing with new places, spaces, and in this case new cities.

As embodied encounters for us humans, such cities are complex, often difficult to experience for the newcomer, but also extraordinary places of joy and freedom. Thessaloniki in Northern Greece is a particular example of such a place, steeped in multicultural history and plural languages and cultures. I have been lucky to both holiday and to work there over time.

This poem originated on one of their public buses, a very hot environment with no air conditioning on this Thursday early afternoon in July, 2022. On this bus, 'we are all intimates' – there is a juxtaposition here of public and of private. To cry in public is perhaps the most vulnerable of acts. Just as our hands can write, so too they can caress, even strangers - *my hands cup his tears like a chalice*. We have a moment of shared relationship ('He says *efcharisto*' [thanks]) but there can be no happy ending in this context; *his lament is continuous*.

Verlaine/Television Haikus

'Chirp-chirp, the birds/ They're giving you the words/ The world is just a feeling you undertook'. *Television* 'Prove It', *Marquee Moon* (words and music: Tom Verlaine).

1
Tom plays guitar
From outer space
Makes poetry noise

2
Thunders was a junkie
Thunders was a sweetie
Johnny sadly had to die

3
Hell is other people
Or Richard with a bass
And the first punk haircut

4
Debbie was a cutie
Debbie was a blondie
With a squeaky voicey

5
Joey got the sneakers
Is seven feet tall
On a telegraph pole droll

6
Marquee Moon closes eyes
To stare at the inner life
Before the world is even open
7
Mapplethorpe did the album
Tom with a middle parting
Patti Smith was jealous of him
8
Hell met Ginsberg
On the LES tenement stairs
Tripped broken rodent steps
9
If Verlaine was a punk vocal
With Baudelaire on bass
His lover Rimbaud on lead
10
Landing at Thessaloniki
I note Venus de Milo singing
A Symbolist poet is wringing

Lucifer Haikus

Hear hear Sartre
holler that the writer
ain't no dirty liar

Into Hell we gotta
stumble like Rimbaud
who found Beauty bitter

But clamber also outta
on the steps and shaky ladder
past Burroughs with his junky bother

And Ginsberg there
to share the East Side flat
with Richard bare

Of food and water
hear hear the punks
holler that truth's no more

But Nihilism's better
L'enfer! L'enfer!

When I Think Of Putin

I think of the Zoo

That is Society

I think of the Thugs

Released from Jail

Who somehow thought

That fighting for Russia

Would be better

Than a life of Imprisonment

As the Moon turns Red

And Madness shows its hand

To Man

Remember this – Putin too

Must face his own Nothingness

A Fall Afternoon

After Gyula Illyés

The Coventry sky that foul day

Was extra grey, so sparing with its light.

It was as if Autumn took the remains of the bright

Blue of summer and spat it out on the side of

The suburban footpath, as coarse as an unswallowed fellatio.

Those patches of little fragile flowers all along the broken roads

Of Tile Hill, in decline since Thatcher's War. Where you trample

The last surviving shoots down with your sexy leather boots in

The rush to get back home quicker. What sardonic laughter

You must have enjoyed together. Three's a crowd. The theatre in the

Sky keeps us mere bystanders bewitched and entranced. Me sitting

In a chair in the corner of our bedroom watching it all slowly unravel.

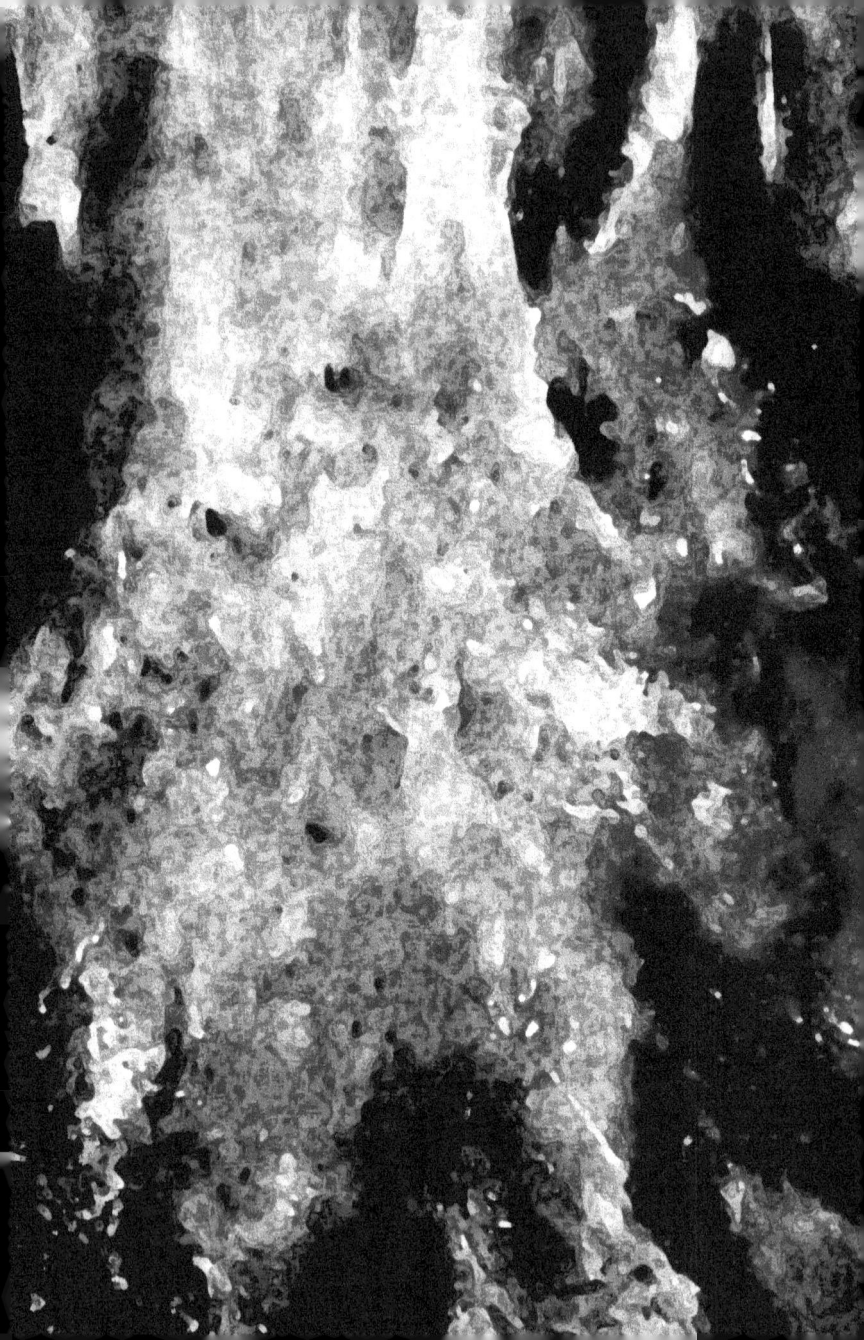

Deep Image or A Painting by Jeffrey Dahmer

Is it true that Jerome Rothenberg

came up with the concept of 'deep image'

after he wilfully opened a large pomegranate in his kitchen

and the blood splattered across the four walls

like a painting by Jeffrey Dahmer?

Francis Bacon Study #1

After Clayton Eshelman

The limits of Bacon's commitment

To the truth of his own experience:

No scenes of cocksucking.

Still, we know that Francis

Studied Police photos. Thus,

We do get the Muriel Belcher

Battered face. We get George

Pye as a Hitlerian boxer

And we get the Realism

Of bux men in tight underwear.

The Librarian

The librarian

from Wroclaw

sent me a photo

of herself semi-

nude lying on a

recliner. I told her

she reminded me

of a *fille de joie*

from one of Bataille's

inter-war novels. She

responded by saying

that she found dissident

Surrealism a bit of a

storm in a tea-cup.

Francis Bacon Study #2

Portrait of George Dyer

His doomed lover

Replaces cure-for-cancer

Hobbies Nietzsche and champagne

Bullfight cut-outs in pulp magazines

An Anglo-Irish painter without a tradition

The Coach and Horses

I used to sit there up

at the barstool looking

at the photographs of

Jeffrey Bernard in mirror

reflection. Every so often

Francis Bacon would arrive

usually Tuesday evenings

which felt incongruous

as you'd be sitting there

with the 20th Century's

greatest artist and literally

the place would be empty.

He would wax lyrical then silence.

Also, he'd been dead for years.

Housmans Bookshop Haiku

No to gentri-catastrophe

Books have soul at London

King's Cross – not for sale

Portrait de Madeleine Riffaud

After a drawing by Picasso, November 1944

At just nineteen

You shot and killed a Nazi

Near *Le Louvre*

Arrested and tortured

You escaped the *Gestapo*

By jumping a train

Once again they recaptured you

Sentenced you to death

But the Liberation was just as abrupt

On August 19, 1944

You reentered Paris

A free woman

In Picasso's *The Clenched Fist*

We see your courageous face

Your long black hair is your valour

Tragic Optimism

With Char, we can see

The world in ruins

Destruction by our own minds

Or hands

As with the two traitors he

Had to execute as part

Of leading the Resistance

Whilst knowing that this

Would come back to haunt

And yet to continue to create

To see your own soul as a double

Often acting even against itself

To accept your responsibility

To seek to own up to your innermost bad faith

Whilst remaining optimistic that there is a path

To write